BUILT

BEFORE THE FLOOD

BUILT
BEFORE THE FLOOD

The Problem
of the
Tiahuanaco Ruins

by

H. S. Bellamy

THE BOOK TREE
San Diego, California

First published
1943
Faber and Faber Limited
London

This revised and enlarged edition
published 1947
All rights reserved

Additional material and revisions
© 2019
The Book Tree

ISBN 978-1-58509-396-0

Cover art
©
Cory Smith

Published by
The Book Tree
P O Box 16476
San Diego, CA 92176
www.thebooktree.com

We provide fascinating and educational products to help awaken the public to new ideas and
information that would not be available otherwise.
Call 1 (800) 700-8733 for our *FREE BOOK TREE CATALOG*.

FOREWORD TO THE SECOND EDITION

The publication of this book has caused considerable interest in wide circles, in spite of the fact that the Tiahuanaco culture is very little known, and that the Theory which has been employed to explain its enigmas is still very unfamiliar.

During the three years since the book was first published research has gone on, and the result is this revised edition. Its chief feature is the newly drafted chapter on the Calendar of Kalasasaya. This was partly necessary because a thorough re-analysis of the symbolism of the Calendar had revealed many new aspects, and partly because a new collaborator, Mr. F. L. Ashton, was able to put the calendar system of the Tiahuanacans upon a stable basis. His valuable contribution has been incorporated in the chapter on the Calendar.

However, both the analysis of the symbolism and its evaluation still require much concentrated and detached thought. I invite all readers of this book to help in puzzling out the points which are as yet hidden.

The plans for the Tiahuanaco Expedition have not made much headway yet. I take this opportunity of thanking my readers and correspondents for the fine interest they have shown, but the financial problem still remains essentially unsolved. Perhaps this new edition will recruit more sponsors.

PREFACE

The Tiahuanaco Problem constitutes one of the most tantalizing major enigmas of our world. It is the more perplexing, therefore, that the number of those who are actively working for its solution is small.

The Tiahuanaco Problem is actually a vast, intimately and intricately interrelated group of problems. Hence the first approach must be general, not special. The whole range of questions must be marshalled in conspectus and a leading line for their solution laid down. Only then can the individual special questions be dealt with by the various branches of science concerned—geography, geophysics, hydrology, geology; biology, œcology, palaeontology, anthropology; archaeology, architecture, technology; mythology, philology; astronomy; etc.

Hitherto the Tiahuanaco Problem has been approached from practically one angle only—that of archaeology—and even this only in a very desultory manner. The various findings have served only to deepen the mystery which enshrouds the enigmatic remains of culture in the Bolivian Altiplano.

The attempt which has been made in this book to propose a general basis for further special work may be considered bold —but in the opinion of the writer it was necessary. It has been made by him since no-one else seemed ready to make it.

The author of this book has never been to the Bolivian Altiplano. It may seem preposterous, therefore, that he should undertake to present a conspectus of the Tiahuanaco Problem, and to suggest a general line of approach as well as to propose a few explanations or interpretations of some of the special questions.

Yet few people have visited Tiahuanaco hitherto. In further exculpation the author wishes to say that he has taken a deep interest in the problems of Tiahuanaco for a great number of years, and has had contact and correspondence with people who are familiar with the site. He knows the literature and has studied numerous photographs, rubbings, and casts of the antiquities of Tiahuanaco, as well as the ground-plans of the ruins. Regarding his interpretations of the peculiar aspects of the Tiahuanaco culture, and especially of the calendar system of the Tiahuanacans, to which the more important, and authoritative, part of this book is devoted, he has been helped, and inspired, partly directly by the applications of a new Cosmological Theory, shortly set forth in this book, and partly by the invaluable findings of Professor Arthur Posnansky, the greatest authority on the antiquities of Tiahuanaco, and of Edmund Kiss, the first successful analyst of the Calendar of Kalasasaya.

Finally, he believes he has some right to speak about the Riddle of Tiahuanaco because he was actually about to join an expedition for the exploration of the Bolivian Altiplano, and had thoroughly prepared himself in all the theoretical aspects of that work. The outbreak of the war prevented this group from assembling and setting out.

Now that this world-wide struggle is over it is hoped that new patrons will come forth to help a new band of explorers to go out to Bolivia. The world needs new and nobler interests, as far removed as possible in time, and in space, from the problems of the post-war years. One of the finest chances is offered by extensive and intensive fieldwork at the yet far too little known and unjustly neglected, but surpassingly interesting, site of Tiahuanaco.

CONTENTS

————————◦———————

NOTE TO THE READER

Diagrams 1, 3, and 11 appeared in color in earlier versions of this work. They were unable to be reproduced in color here, which makes the references to colors, which accompany the diagrams, obsolete. The reader can still understand what is being discussed by paying special attention to the level of shading found in these diagrams.

Diagrams 14-19 also displayed a singular, darker (muddy orange) color in earlier printings. In this edition it is clearly seen as darker in black and white, and easy to interpret, should reference be made.

The Book Tree

DIAGRAMS

The diagrams of the sculptures on the Calendar Gate were drawn by the author from special rubbings and casts.

1

THE INTER-ANDEAN ALTIPLANO

In the heart of the Andes, surrounded by lofty mountain-chains, there is situated, at an average height of 12,300 feet above sea-level, the most elevated lacustrine basin in the world: the Altiplano, or Meseta, of Bolivia. There at one time, in the dim past, one of the most remarkable cultures which man ever evolved had its home—and found its tomb.

The Meseta now contains slightly brackish Lake Titicaca,[1] which measures 110 by 35 miles, salty Lake Poöpo (about 50 by 20 miles), briny Lake Coipasa (about 20 by 10 miles), and extensive saline marshes and salt-deserts—but at certain times in the past sheets of water differing in level and extent must have existed in the Bolivian Tableland. (Cf. the Map facing page 14.)

From various evidence it appears that the waters in the Altiplano reached three distinct levels. At the earliest, and lowest, stage there seems to have existed a lake which was probably considerably smaller than Lake Titicaca; but when, after an important intermediary stage, the waters reached their highest level, they filled the whole Altiplano and covered an area measuring about 460 miles in length and from 30 to over 100 miles in width: a veritable 'Inter-Andean Sea'. Finally the present state was reached, which is practically one of slow desiccation.

The intermediary and highest stages of the 'Inter-Andean Sea' have left distinct ancient strandlines at two levels above the surface of Lake Titicaca. These former littorals, and their peculiarities, and the problems they present, will be discussed further in the following pages.

13

The earliest, lowest, level of the waters can be inferred from other evidences.

The 'Inter-Andean Sea of the Intermediate Strandline' is— even though only rarely and hazily—referred to in relative literature as 'Lake Minchin' (after the geographer J. B. Minchin who first noticed the calcareous deposits which mark its former littoral); the 'Inter-Andean Sea of the Highest Strandline' is sometimes given the name of 'Lake Ballivián' (after the Bolivian notable, M. V. Ballivián, who was deeply interested in the geography of his country). Little detailed attention has been paid to these strandlines hitherto, however, and practically no conclusions have been drawn as to their relation to the various culture evidences in the Altiplano.

The hydrography of the Inter-Andean Lacustrine Basin is very puzzling. As this Basin is self-contained its waters can only be derived from the precipitation in its catchment area. At

---

DIAGRAM 1

The map opposite shows, in darker blue, the present lakes in the Bolivian Altiplano: Titicaca and Poöpo, connected by the Desaguadero, as well as marshy Coipasa which is seasonally replenished with water through the Lacahahuira. This state is practically the same as the Stage of the Lowest Level. Mountains of a height of more than 14,000 feet above present sea-level are shown in brown; this is the territory above the Highest Strandline which was probably never submerged. The white space inside this barrier practically corresponds to the Stage of the Highest Level, whose waters, at the La Paz and Ascotan Gaps, were in connection with the girdle-tide, which is typified by the white space outside the mountain barrier. In between these two Levels there was the Inter-Andean Sea of the Intermediate Level on whose shore Tiahuanaco was situated. Its approximate extent is here shown in light blue. (Cf. also the diagram of the Ideal Longitudinal Section through the Bolivian Altiplano, facing page 58).

14

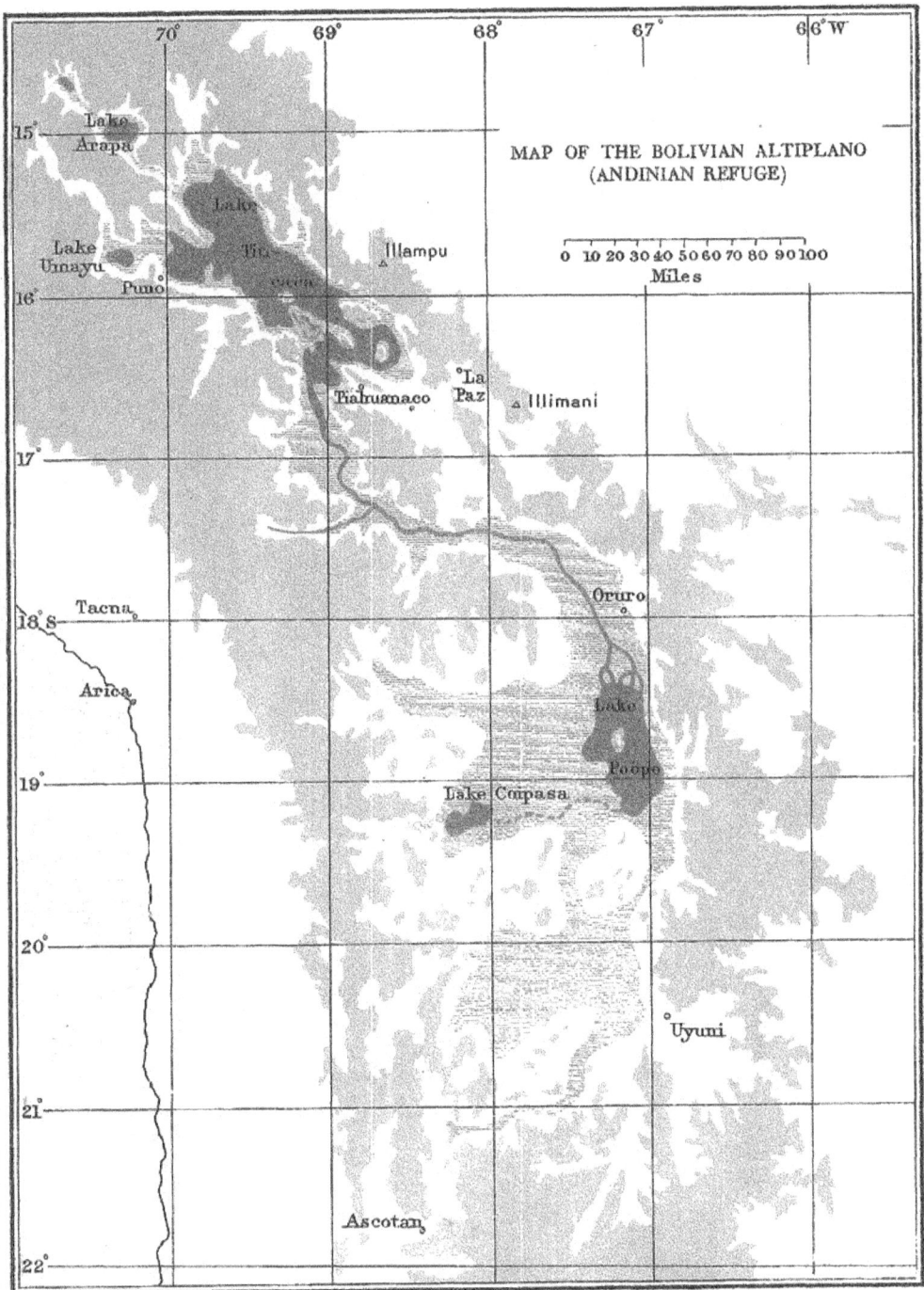

MAP OF THE BOLIVIAN ALTIPLANO
(ANDINIAN REFUGE)

0 10 20 30 40 50 60 70 80 90 100
Miles

Lake
Arapa

15°

Lake

Lake
Umayu

Puno

16°

Illampu

Tiahuanaco

°La
Paz

Illimani

17°

Oruro

Tacna

18°S

Arica

Lake
Poopo

19°

Lake Copasa

20°

Uyuni

21°

Ascotan

22°

70°   69°   68°   67°   66°W

Stanford, London

present, gain by precipitation and loss by evaporation, and other causes, are practically balanced. The meteorological conditions, therefore, which must be presupposed in order to explain the coming into existence, and the maintenance, of the vast sheets of water revealed by the intermediary and highest strandlines, are almost inconceivable—if, indeed, meteorological conditions were really responsible for the palaeo-hydrography of that region.

As the rise from the lowest level to the intermediary, and from the intermediary to the highest, seems to have been 'sudden', it has been suggested that at two periods in the past an enormous glaciation of the Andes must have broken down owing to a change of climate.

Another, and even greater, problem is presented by the saltiness of the lakes in the Meseta, and especially by the presence of the great saline deserts of the whole region. Lake Titicaca (12,506 feet above sea-level; up to 890 feet deep) is slightly brackish. Lake Poöpo, situated about 180 miles to the southeast, at a height of 12,051 feet above sea-level, obtains its water from Lake Titicaca through the sluggish[2] Desaguadero River (length about 220 miles); its greatest depth is only about nine feet and its water is so salty that any fishes reaching it from Lake Titicaca do not seem to be able to propagate in it. Lake Poöpo seeps[3] seasonally towards the west through the Lacahahuira 'River' (length about 65 miles) into the shallow and marshy, and very briny, Lake Coipasa (12,051 feet above sea-level), which has no outlet: the water evaporates, or sinks into the ground. Lake Coipasa is situated at the northern extremity of the Salt-Desert of Coipasa (the dried up part of the lake) which measures about 50 by 35 miles. Farther to the south still is the extensive Salt-Plain of Uyuni, measuring about 80 by 70 miles, and situated slightly over 12,000 feet above sea-level. It is joined in the south-west by a long chain of small salt, saltpetre, and borax, lakes and pans, situated in a winding valley about a hundred miles in length, but only from 5 to 8 miles wide.

15

The region in which the feeders of Lake Titicaca rise consists almost exclusively of old crystalline, and younger volcanic, rocks; triassic formations, from which salt is usually derived through extraction, are markedly absent. Hence the presence of so much salt in the Bolivian Tableland can only be accounted for by postulating a former connexion of the great lacustrine basin with the Ocean, and by assuming the eventual evaporation of this body of water when the connexion with the Ocean was at last severed.

However, to fill the Inter-Andean Altiplano to the level of the highest ancient strandline observed there, and to make the former 'Inter-Andean Sea' a communicating part of the Ocean, the continent of South America must have been at least 13,000 feet lower—or, what amounts to the same, the level of the Ocean must have been at least 13,000 feet higher.

Even then the connexion with the Ocean would only have been effected at three places, and through very narrow defiles: in the north-east of the Bolivian Basin, near La Paz, where there is a narrow pass about 12,800 feet above sea-level; in the south-west, near Ascotan, where there is the long narrow defile mentioned above, about 12,400 feet above sea-level; and in the south-east, near Uyuni, where there is a col about 12,800 feet above sea-level.[4] Everywhere else the Altiplano is surrounded by a mountain-wall over 14,000 feet high.

The chief idea current at the present time is that towards the end of the Tertiary Age a small 'Andean Continent' was raised some 13,000 feet out of the waters of the ocean by powers working from within the Earth. This 'rise' also caused the emergence of the foot, or shelf, of the former small continent, which became the present extensive Continent of South America. This theory has been advanced, and accepted, only because it is evidently impossible to presuppose an ocean, of necessity world-wide, whose level was 13,000 feet higher than at present, or, rather, to account for the apparently sudden disappearance of the volume of water between that former

16

level of the Ocean and the present. Matters would be greatly simplified, of course, if it were possible to presuppose not a general but only a 'local', and 'temporary', change in the level of the Ocean. In other words: if it could be shown that at a certain period in the past the waters of the Ocean had been redistributed for a time—withdrawn from the higher latitudes and 'piled up' in the tropical zone of the Earth, so to speak—the Continental Uplift Theory could be liquidated and many formidable problems could be approached from another, and possibly more promising, angle.

Such a redistribution of the waters of the terrestrial Ocean might come about in two ways.—If the Earth increased its speed of rotation, the waters would rise in the tropical belt and eventually form a sort of water-girdle there. But, as a force which might urge on the rotation of the Earth sufficiently is inconceivable, this explanation is impossible. However, a tropical water-girdle would also come into existence if an extra-terrestrial force acted upon the waters of the Ocean. A force of that kind is readily conceivable: the gravitational pull of a Satellite.

2

COSMOLOGICAL CONSIDERATIONS

———————◦———————

At this point it may be well worth while to interrupt our investigation into the problems of the Inter-Andean Altiplano, and of the riddle of Tiahuanaco, in order to get as clear a conception as possible of the tidal phenomenon postulated at the end of the first chapter and of its causation.

Our Earth is accompanied on its journey round the Sun by a Satellite, the Moon. How our planet obtained this companion is not known; the only certain thing is that it has not been with the Earth from the very beginning. Speculation as to its origin, or derivation, reveals two possibilities.

The first possibility is that the Moon is a child of the Earth, and that it was thrown off by centrifugal forces in an exceedingly remote age when our planet was still a ball of fluid (or semi-fluid) glowing cosmic material, which for some reason or other speeded up its rotation sufficiently for a time to allow the escape of material at its equator.

The other possibility is that the Moon was originally an independent sister planet of the Earth's which was 'captured' by our Earth at a time not necessarily very remote.

It would appear that the latter possibility is much more likely from every point of view.

So much for the past of the Moon. Its future is an equally interesting subject for speculation. Again there are two possibilities.

Either the Moon, no matter how acquired, will always remain the Satellite of our Earth—or it will not.

It will be admitted that the second possibility seems, on the face of it, to be the more probable. If this is so—what will be the end of the Moon? Once more there are two possibilities.

Will our Satellite move farther and farther away from the Earth, and at last be lost when the gravitational tie snaps? Or will it come nearer and nearer, and eventually disintegrate, its material showering down on the Earth?

Again the latter possibility seems much more likely. It would, indeed, be the logical continuation and end of the process which led to the capture of the planet Luna.

If our present Moon will eventually crumble into fragments and crash down on the Earth, it would be interesting to consider the further question—whether Luna is the one and only satellite our planet has ever had, or will ever have, or whether our Moon has had a predecessor, or, indeed, more than one, and whether it will have any successor, or successors.

To attempt a reply which may be very near the truth is quite within the reach of possibility.

The capture of a smaller planet by a bigger would result when the smaller trespasses into the active gravitational realm of the bigger. An orbital disturbance of that kind might be due to 'acute' or to 'chronic' outside influences.

A sudden disturbance might be caused by the passage of a cosmic body, foreign to our Solar System, which was powerful enough to distort the planetary orbits, but not powerful enough to bring about a complete collapse of the Solar System. However, the instance is practically hypothetical, because 'errant' bodies of planetary size do not seem to exist in space, or, if they do, they will be exceedingly rare, while the frequent visitors from without, comets and meteorites, are too minute of mass to cause any sort of orbital disturbance.

A slow, disturbing influence would be effected by the resistance offered by a 'cosmic medium'. The orbits of bodies revolving in an 'unideal space' would not be re-entering curves (ellipses), but ellipsoidal inward-tending spirals. The 'pitch' of these orbital spirals, or, in other words, the speed of involution, would depend, partly, on the density of the cosmic, or inter-planetary, medium and partly on the size, mass, and speed, of each body revolving in it.

Interstellar, and especially interplanetary, space cannot be absolutely vacuous. Our Sun continuously exhales gases, chiefly hydrogen, as well as impalpably fine (subatomary, atomary, and molecular) material, and all stars ceaselessly do the same.

The pressure of light carries these gaseous and other ex-halations away out into the abysses of space. Naturally this material medium will be densest in the neighbourhood of the Sun (and the other stars), probably decreasing in density with the cube of the distance.

The bigger and more massive a planetary body is, and the more quickly it moves through the interplanetary medium, the smaller its degree of involution will be; a smaller, lighter, and more slowly moving body, on the other hand, will experience a greater diminution of its orbit, for smaller bodies have a larger resistance-experiencing surface compared with their resistance-opposing mass and orbital momentum.

Hence any smaller, lighter planet swinging round the Sun outside a bigger, more massive one must, in the course of time, trespass into its active gravitational sphere and, of course, eventually be captured and made into a Satellite.

From this it follows that our Moon must have once been a transterrestrial, independent planet, and that its predecessors, if any, must also have been derived from that region of planetary space. A further consequence is that, after the end of our present companion, the planet Mars, which is considerably smaller than the Earth, will eventually become our Satellite—unless it is too massive to be captured. In such a case it will spiral 'beyond' the Earth, after a series of devastating close conjunctions.

The theory of an 'unideal' space, and its various far-reaching astrophysical consequences, forms part of the teachings of the Viennese cosmologist, Hans Hoerbiger (1860-1931).

COSMOLOGICAL CONSIDERATIONS

Readers interested in a fuller exposition are referred to the present writer's book, *Moons, Myths, and Man*, in which appears the only summary of this theory hitherto published in English, or to Hoerbiger's original work (written in German) mentioned in the Bibliography. Here reference will be made only to certain relevant points of this theory, which bear on the helicoidal diminution or involution of the orbits of planetary and satellitic bodies.

The helicoidal orbital diminution which has made a small, outer planet the satellite of an inner, bigger one, continues, of course, after the capture. For relative to the Sun the intercepted planet retains its original orbit: only it has become intertwined with its captor's and has now the shape of a very shallow, helicoidal, undulating curve.[5] Thus eventually the companion gets into so close a proximity to its gravitational master that it begins to disintegrate, and then its debris showers down in a hail of blazing blocks.

Before it acquired—possibly quite 'recently'—the planet Luna as its Satellite, our Earth may have had at least half a dozen other companions in the course of its history. We cannot enter here upon a discussion of the proofs which Hoerbiger very convincingly puts forward in support of this assertion. This must be reserved for a special monograph. In what follows we shall pursue the influence the predecessor of our present companion had upon our Earth. (This, of course, will be more or less valid for our Moon also.)

As our Moon does now, its predecessor, when at a comparable distance,[6] caused two 'tide-humps' in the waters of the Ocean. One, the 'zenithal tide-hump', was formed immediately under the Satellite, through its gravitational pull. Diametrically opposite to this there was the 'nadiral tide-hump', which came into existence through the swing of the system Earth : Satellite round its common centre (cf. Note 5). The nearer the Satellite approached and the more powerful its gravitational pull consequently grew, the higher these tide-humps became. More and more water was drawn into the

21

tropics from the higher northern and southern latitudes. Owing to the inertia of the waters the two great tide-humps actually took the form rather of a sort of annular 'tide-bulge'. This 'tide-bulge', an early form of the 'girdle-tide' to be mentioned later, submerged most of the lower-lying land-areas in the tropics. The more elevated parts of the continents continued to exist as big islands in these slowly rising waters.

To these 'refuges' all land-life withdrew. In the high and middle latitudes of the Earth vast land-areas emerged, but they were not inhabitable because the approaching Satellite also drew the protective air-blanket of our planet towards the tropics. So while it was probably even warmer in the tropics then than it is now, it was excessively cold even in the middle latitudes. Any water remaining there was frozen, and any meteorological precipitation added to this glaciation. The fringe of the polar ice-caps spread far into the latitudes now called temperate, and glacier fingers here and there may have approached even the shores of the great girdle-tide.

The nearer the Satellite spiralled, the more quickly it moved round the Earth, and the shorter, consequently, became the 'month', that is, one complete revolution of the Satellite round our planet. As long as the Satellite took more than one day for one complete revolution, the great Satellite-caused and Satellite-controlled tide-bulge acted like a sort of band (or strap) brake and hence slowed up the rotation of the Earth. Thus the length of the 'day' increased, probably quite appreciably, as time went on.

When the length of the 'month' approached that of the 'day', the waters of the Earth gathered into two huge, separate tide-hills—one immediately underneath the Satellite, and the other diametrically opposite. It so happened that the Satellite became 'stationary' over Africa, which is the 'heaviest' part of the terrestrial surface and was therefore able to 'hold' the Satellite. The 'zenithal tide-hill', the one under the Satellite, was therefore vaulted over Africa and the 'nadiral tide-hill', on the opposite side of our planet, filled the area now taken up by the Pacific Ocean. (Hoerbiger mentions interesting proofs for this contention of his.) This 'age of the one day month' happened when the Satellite was only about six terrestrial radii away from our Earth (centre to centre distance).

Eventually the Satellite began to outspeed the rotation of the Earth—the 'month' became shorter than the day! The two

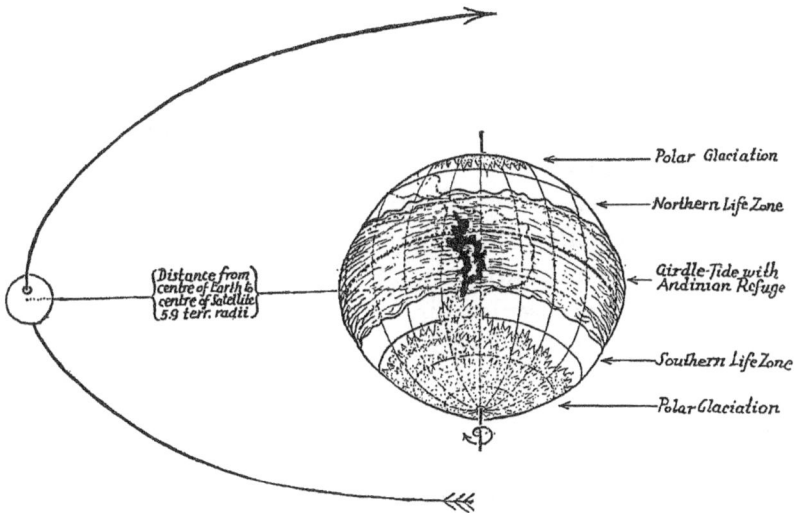

Distance from centre of Earth to centre of Satellite 5.9 terr. radii

— Polar Glaciation

— Northern Life Zone

Girdle-Tide with Andinian Refuge

— Southern Life Zone

— Polar Glaciation

DIAGRAM 2

The Earth and its Satellite at the time of Tiahuanaco

tide-hills, too, moved forward with the Satellite, and became the more elongated the more quickly the Satellite moved. Finally the head of the one caught up with the tail of the other and eventually a great Earth-encircling water-ring, the 'girdle tide', developed. (Cf. Diagram 2.) This 'girdle-tide' was much narrower and higher than the tide-bulge mentioned above, because of the much greater nearness of the Satellite. Furthermore, now that the Satellite moved more quickly than the Earth rotated, it carried the tide-ring which

23

it controlled along with it, and the waters in their turn 'took along' the Earth with them. Henceforth the terrestrial rotation was being speeded up, and the length of the day began to decrease slowly.

The actual existence of this girdle-tide is proved by the highly elevated shorelines and beaches which are observable in 'tropical' districts, as well as by the greatly denuded and abraded areas of the Earth within that zone.

In its earlier stages the girdle-tide rose more quickly, as the waters were able to obey the Satellite's gravitational pull rather freely; at last, however, a height was reached beyond which, for physical reasons, the waters could not rise, even though the gravitational power of the Satellite kept increasing with its incessant approach.

The gathering waters of the girdle-tide urged some of the tribes who inhabited the living space then available to move north, and others south, out of the equatorial belt and the tropics, in a slow, secular flight. This 'flight' was probably so slow as to be quite imperceptible to the 'refugees'. Generation after generation found the sea encroach upon their land, and slowly withdrew before the rising waters—much as people do now in the coastal districts of certain parts of Britain and elsewhere. Many tribes, of course, remained in certain tropical land areas, but they were forced to climb higher and higher up the mountain-slopes, as generation after generation passed. Unless they could escape by means of some sort of craft, certain tribes which found themselves in unfavourably situated regions, in areas which proved too low, were drowned out of existence in their 'sinking' islands. But also the refugees in apparently favourable situations were not absolutely safe: a slight shift of the 'axis' of the girdle-tide owing to a 'precessional' wobble of our planet may have caused them suddenly to become veritable death-traps.

The chief tropical 'island-refuges' set in the girdle-tide were, probably, 'Andinia', Mexico, Abyssinia, Tibet, and New Guinea. To the discussion of some of the problems connected with the Refuge of 'Andinia' this treatise is devoted.

In the last stage of its existence, the predecessor of our Moon approached so close that the disruptive forces of the terrestrial gravitation outweighed the cohesive powers of the Satellite, and it disintegrated. This probably happened when the centre to centre distance of the Earth and the Satellite was only about 1·8 terrestrial radii (Roche's 'critical distance'). For a short time a ring of satellitic debris encircled the Earth, somewhat resembling (though not as to material, density, and mass) the similarly engendered ring of Saturn. Being relatively small, these fragments spiralled quickly down to the surface of the Earth. A comparatively narrow zone of our planet, which more or less coincided with the area covered by the girdle-tide, was exposed to this terrific cosmic bombardment. Most of the big fragments into which the Satellite was riven plunged deep below the Earth's surface. Most of the smaller ones were washed or carried away by the waters when the girdle-tide eventually broke up.

As soon as the pull of the disintegrating Satellite had sufficiently waned, the waters of the girdle-tide began to flow, surge, race off north and south in a series of gigantic ring-waves. Now the narrow tropical island refuges rose out of the waters and expanded into wide continents: Andinia became South America, Abyssinia Africa, etc. Soon the survivors of the cataclysm took possession of this new life-space.

In the higher latitudes north and south, on the other hand, the waters rose and submerged much land; but there were few inhabitants, or none, to suffer in these regions.

Needless to say, also the atmosphere was thrown into confusion during the breakdown cataclysm of the Satellite.

Earthquakes rocked the whole planet once the distortive influence of the Satellite's gravitation was at an end, and the flattened Earth was free to return to its spherical shape.

After the end of the Companion, an asatellitic, or moonless, aeon started for our Earth. It was a great age of recuperation in which life rallied for an ascent to new heights of development.

During all this aeon the planet Luna kept drawing nearer and nearer. Eventually it was near enough for its gravitational powers to draw the waters of the Earth's seas slightly towards the tropics. At every conjunction then a small tidal catastrophe happened in the equatorial zone of the Earth. At last the critical conjunction occurred: Luna was deprived of its independence, and became the Satellite of our Earth. Then a major catastrophe swept our planet: the capture cataclysm. Extensive land areas in the tropics were permanently submerged by the shallow beginnings of a new 'tide-bulge'; earthquakes shook our planet, which became slightly more flattened again; the equilibrium of the atmosphere was upset.

The most favourable relative position for the capture of a smaller outer planet as a satellite occurs when the smaller outer planet is at its perihelion, and the bigger inner one is at its aphelion. Then not only are the two able to approach most closely, but also the slower outer planet moves at its quickest while the quicker inner one moves at its slowest. Indeed, the two bodies may be moving, for a certain time, in practically parallel paths at practically the same speed. The gravitational powers which the two neighbours then excited upon one another caused the orbits of both the Earth and of Luna to become more eccentric. At every conjunction the place of the terrestrial aphelion was being pulled slightly (theoretically one unit) farther outwards, while the place of the lunar perihelion was being pulled considerably farther inwards (theoretically 80 units—the relative masses of the Moon and the Earth being about 1 : 80). Finally, perhaps even before the last exact meeting of the inverse apsides, so close a conjunction resulted that Luna was altogether pulled out of its independent planetary path and its orbit entwined itself with the Earth's in the shape of the undulating curve before mentioned.

It is not (yet) possible to say even approximately when the

predecessor of our present Moon came to its end, or when the planet Luna was forced to become the companion of our Earth. Tentatively the capture of the Moon may be put somewhere near 11,500 B.C., a figure which probably will not need a very drastic revision. The breakdown of the Moon's predecessor, however, certainly did not happen less than 250,000 years ago.

Though any exact dating or timing is not yet possible, one thing may be considered as certain: even during the aeon of the predecessor of our present Moon, Man was already what he is now—an artist, a scientist, an observer and recorder of facts, a social and political being: in short, he was *homo sapiens*. This statement is well based on certain cultural remains, and certain palaeontological evidences, which seem to speak authoritatively for our view. And it is powerfully supported by the Myths— those strangely persistent, and insistent, reports of deluges, and fire-hail, and world-wide catastrophe, which are current even among 'primitive' peoples. Though they may be frowned upon as witnesses, many of them contain certain statements of fact, and descriptions of certain sequences of events, which could not possibly have been 'invented',[7] and they may well help to open a vista into the darkness which bounds the ken of our historical horizon.

It may be admitted that a trend of thought like that just outlined might help to explain many of the problems connected with the Altiplano of Bolivia, the Inter-Andean Sea and its peculiarities, and give the reason why a high culture of so singular a type is found in those uplands. It is therefore suggested that we should try an approach from this angle.

3

AN ANCIENT REFUGE OF MAN

———————⟶◦⟵———————

To return to our main subject: 'Andinia'—i.e. the great Bolivian Altiplano and the mountainous regions of Bolivia, Peru, Chile, and the Argentine which surround it—was one of the refuges, or asylums, of Mankind at the time of the great girdle-tide.[8] Because of its high elevation—its lowest part is about 12,000 feet above the present sea-level—it seemed to be an absolutely 'safe' asylum where mankind could get through the great time of cosmic stress. Nevertheless catastrophe seems to have overtaken parts of 'Andinia' at certain times—at least twice, if we interpret evidences aright.

In the days of the great girdle-tide, Andinia consisted of a vast plain (the present Inter-Andean Meseta or Altiplano) surrounded by walls of frequently multiple mountain-ranges which rose, in certain peaks, to about 10,000 feet above the average level of the Meseta, if viewed from within the Asylum, and to slightly more 'above sea-level', i.e. above the then level of the girdle-tide in that zone, if viewed from without. The great plain, therefore, was for the greater part of it situated well above the waters of the girdle-tide, in which the whole large island, or small continent, of the Refuge of Andinia was set. The Inter-Andean plain was apparently well watered and contained a number of (sweet-water) lakes, the largest of which, the predecessor of Lake Titicaca, was somewhat lower, and hence also smaller, than the present lake.

At, or near, the shore of that 'Lake Pre-Titicaca', unknown peoples built substantial, roughly orientated temples for their gods, and habitations of wrought stone for themselves.

Whether these builders were indigenous to the Inter-Andean Region, or whether they were refugees, driven there from the lower parts of the outer Andes by the rising waters of the girdle-tide, we cannot now establish. Nor is the question important.

These settlers of the age of the lowest water-level in the Bolivian Meseta, or Asylum of Andinia, built the settlements of Huacullani and of Simillake, and several others, among them also that of which the remains (the so-called 'Old Temple', for instance) have been discovered below the 'classic' culture-stratum of Tiahuanaco.

We do not, of course, know anything at all about the actual names of these settlements. Huacullani is so called here because its much-weathered ruins can be seen partly to emerge in the neighbourhood of the present village of Huacullani in the shallow shore-parts of the Bight of Apachete de Tambillo of Lake Titicaca, when the waters are exceptionally low at some seasons. The ruins of Simillake have been given their name because they are situated on the island of Simillake, in the Bight of Jaconta Palayani, the southernmost part of Lake Titicaca, where the Desaguadero River leaves it. These ruins lie slightly (about three feet) below the present average level of Lake Titicaca.[9]

The architectural remains of this 'First Period' show the following common—and peculiar—traits: The walls of certain of the edifices (such as those of Simillake) are sometimes as much as ten feet thick; the builders always seem to have sunk the floors of their edifices well below the ground-level; the stones of which these half-sunk edifices were built are worked on five sides only, the sixth, which was in contact with the soil, remaining rough; while the smaller edifices may have been covered, the larger ones (such as the 'Old Temple' of Tiahuanaco, which measures about 90 by 100 feet) can never have had roofs; the material used is practically always a stratified reddish sandstone which was broken in quarries in the vicinity of the settlements and worked probably with copper tools.

AN ANCIENT REFUGE OF MAN

While the settlements of Huacullani, Simillake, etc., must have been situated at, or near, the shore of 'Lake Pre-Titicaca', and were built there probably for reasons of industry or commerce, the settlement of which the 'Old Temple' of Tiahuanaco was the centre was built about 13 or 14 miles away from that Lake, and the reason for its having been sited there is not manifest. Evidently it was a centre of importance, but it was not built in the 'best' place then available. The material of the Old Temple, a red sandstone of the grauwacke type, came almost certainly by land from the range of hills named Quimsachata, where a similar sandstone occurs near the present village of Andamarca, about five miles south of Tiahuanaco. The least unlikely explanation why 'better' sites closer to the quarries were not utilized is that the locality where the Old Temple was built was for some reason or other considered as 'holy'. It evidently remained so at a later period when the Tiahuanaco of the classical period was built on the same site, of material which was transported by water from at least six times as far.

The inhabitants of some at least of the settlements near the lowest water-level in the Bolivian Meseta must have attained to a considerable, if peculiar, standard of culture. This is shown in particular by a strange manner of ornamentation. The lowest courses of the building stones of the walls of the Old Temple, for instance, are adorned with peculiarly arranged sculptured heads which, though very crude in technique, nevertheless seem to attempt to portray different features. The chins of a few of them are so elongated that one is tempted to regard them as depicting bearded faces. They are fixed only about a foot from the floor and may have been placed there for 'magical' reasons, as protectors of the building, perhaps, or of its foundations.

The settlements of the 'First Period' of culture in the Andinian Asylum were overwhelmed by a flood catastrophe.

Usually it is suggested that a great glaciation of the lofty mountain-chains surrounding the Inter-Andean Basin had

30

broken down, and that the torrents descending from the melting ice-caps had caused the level of 'Lake Pre-Titicaca', and that of any other sheets of water then existing in the area of the Meseta, to rise. But even the melting of the most extensive glaciation imaginable would not account for the enormous volume of water which seems to have poured quite *suddenly* into the Great Basin of Andinia, submerged much of its land-area, and formed the 'Inter-Andean Sea of the Intermediate Strandline'. Also the undoubted fact that this new 'Inter-Andean Sea' was *salt* could not be explained by the hypothesis of melting.

The real cause of the flood catastrophe seems to have been this.—The Andinian Refuge had apparently been situated appreciably to the south of the 'axis' of the satellite-caused girdle-tide, i.e. the central belt where the water-ring was highest. The axis of the girdle-tide will not have altogether coincided with the equator, although the tropics of the Satellite must have been rather narrow. Approximately the crest of the great water ring may have been situated between 1100 and 1300 miles to the north of Tiahuanaco. A precessional movement of our Earth[10] had caused the axis of the girdle-tide to shift towards the south. Thus the waters had suddenly 'risen' round Andinia, and the Meseta had 'sunk' below sea-level. Great waves of the girdle-tide, agitated by this sudden axial change, over-leapt certain lower parts of the mountain-ranges which surrounded the Asylum and descended into the Meseta. The waters probably raced in also through the 'weak spots' in the great mountain wall, chiefly through the defile to the west of La Paz, in a lesser degree through the gap to the south of Ascotan, and possibly also through the weak spot east of Uyuni.

It was thus that a vast area of the Inter-Andean Meseta was set under water, and the 'Inter-Andean Sea of the Intermediate Strandline'—a land-locked sea—came into being. (Cf. the Map facing page 14.) It will be appreciated that this explanation bears at least the stamp of possibility.

When the inflow of water eventually stopped, some 90 feet of water covered the settlement of Simillake. Huacullani, and certainly other sites of the First Period, which may yet be discovered, were submerged to a similar depth. The 'Old Temple' of Tiahuanaco, and the settlement near it, having been situated on much higher ground, eventually remained above the new level of the waters, but were filled with mud and shingle[11] thrown there by the waters which rushed into the Asylum. The Old Temple, which had formerly been situated a considerable distance from the shore of 'Lake Pre-Titicaca', now lay immediately at the shore of the new Inter-Andean Sea.

4

THE RISE OF A NEW CULTURE

Though the curtain had fallen on the First Period of the Andinian Culture, the stage was set for a new act. After its great precessional swing southward the axis of the girdle-tide had probably moved northward again in a compensatory oscillation, and for a very long spell of time any subsequent axial changes were evidently not of so determined a nature as to endanger the Andinian Asylum. Hence it 'rose' again, and as no more water lapped over low parts of the surrounding mountain-walls, or raced in through the three 'weak spots', the level of the (land-locked) Inter-Andean Sea became, and remained, stable.

The survivors of the submerged settlements of the First Period would probably have set to work again as soon as they had ascertained that all danger from a repetition of the flood catastrophe had passed. They would have tried to recreate their sturdy, if crude, culture.

But just at that time, immigrants of another, more advanced, race seem to have appeared among the autochthonous survivors of the great inundation catastrophe. They were probably refugees from lost settlements which had perhaps been situated in the lower parts of the (eastern?) outer ranges of the Andinian Asylum. Where they came from—whether their former settlements lie engulfed in primeval forests, or whether they have been utterly destroyed by the waters which dispossessed them—is not known; nor is it material. The wonderfully life-like 'face-urns' of the Second Period of Culture in the Andinian Refuge which was now about to start, and various sculptures, give direct evidence of this immigration by revealing a great variety of racial types. Besides the typical square 'American' face are found purely 'Nordic', slightly mongoloid, and even distinctly negroid types. Also a statue showing a *bearded* individual has been found. Be that as it may, there suddenly become evident the manifold, powerful, expressions of a tremendous and dynamic—a veritably explosive— 'culture-will' in the Andinian Asylum. Though transplanted from elsewhere, probably under the most unfavourable circumstances imaginable, the new culture immediately struck deep root in the Altiplano. The bearers of this culture seem to have set to work with energetic efficiency, and an unflagging determination to overcome all danger and rise over all difficulties. The losses they had sustained through the great flood catastrophe in their former habitations had not disorganized them. They were evidently numerous: it appears as if a whole people, nay, several nations, had packed up and migrated; there can be no doubt that they were highly cultured; of labour skilled and unskilled they seem to have had an almost unlimited supply; transport offered no problems for them; food must have been varied and plentiful.

Under such, or very similar, circumstances the Second Period of Culture in the Andinian Asylum began—the 'Classical Period' of Tiahuanaco, as it has been named from the most important site on the shore of the land-locked Inter-Andean Sea of the Intermediate level—and soon it spread its fertilizing cultural impulses over all the area of the Asylum. This area was probably the mythical land of 'Ttahua-ntin-Suyu', the 'Common Gathering Place of All Nations',[12] of which local Indian tradition is still faintly reminiscent. (Cf. Diagram 3 facing page 36.) So safe did the rulers of that realm feel, that they embarked upon grandiose, ambitious, long-term building schemes for a Sacred Capital, and began to erect extensive, well-orientated edifices. And far from being afraid of the waters, they even made them their servant by building harbours and docks, and their defender by digging a long, canal-like moat (or moat-like canal), which was approximately 100 feet wide.

The new arrivals probably selected the area of the settlement of the 'Old Temple' as the site of their great sacred city, partly because it had been an important spiritual centre before —the ornamental symbolism of the Old Temple definitely points that way—and because the traditional 'holiness' of the territory had been proved by the fact that the terrible waters which had swallowed all the other settlements of the First Period had been unable to engulf it, too. But, partly, the site was chosen probably because of its 'strategic' position and its 'central' situation. For the culture of the Second Period seems to have flourished chiefly in the shore districts of the northernmost part of the Inter-Andean Sea of the Intermediate Level, which could easily be reached from the harbours of Tiahuanaco.

No comparatively soft local sandstone for the builders of the edifices of the Second Period of Tiahuanaco! Though they did not absolutely disdain using it occasionally, they set out to search for the hardest and toughest stone which occurs in the whole region. They eventually found it in the andesite[13] which forms the slopes of the volcano Kappia.[14] The andesite quarries were about 30 miles by water in a straight line from the quays of the new capital, but the builders thought little of distance and of transport difficulties. They broke huge[15] blocks of this volcanic rock and took them, roughly squared, to the masons' yards near their building sites, where they worked and adorned them beautifully, and with a skill rarely paralleled, and perhaps never surpassed, anywhere in the world.

The supreme mastery of the builders of Tiahuanaco over their difficult material has not perhaps been fully appreciated till now. All stones which have somehow escaped bad weathering show an extreme precision of cutting; all surfaces are absolutely plane and finely ground or polished; there are no traces of the chisel; all lines are straight and parallel; all angles are surprisingly true; all measurements are meticulously exact[16]; the edges are clean and sharp.

35

The art of the 'classic' period of Tiahuanaco, that is, the style revealed chiefly by the Calendar Gate of the Temple of Kalasasaya and contemporaneous products of the chisel, is not the beginning, but the culmination, of a line of development. It is the result of a highly developed process of artistic abstraction. There is nothing 'aboriginal' perceivable anywhere in the

---

DIAGRAM 3

This remarkable pictograph adorns the flat top of the tiara-like cap of office of what is evidently a high priestly dignitary of the classic period whose exquisitely painted terracotta head was excavated at Tiahuanaco. According to Posnansky, and others, the meaning of its rich symbolism is unknown. In my opinion, we have before us a highly conventionalized 'Map' of the 'World' known to the inhabitants of the Andinian Life Asylum, which also features certain magical (or 'religious') elements.

The quartering is indicative of the general name of the Andinian Life Asylum, Ttahua-ntin-Suyu (which the Incas eventually arrogated for their empire). This name means, literally translated, 'Four Regions Together', or, freely rendered, 'Common Country of the United Nations of the Four Corners of the World'. The brown 'step-symbol' is the hierograph 'Earth' and is also indicative of the andenes, or agricultural terraces, of the deeply indented Life Asylum which was set in the Girdle-tide. The white circles (actually bosses) at the corners symbolize the snow-capped highest Andean peak in the neighbourhood of Tiahuanaco, perhaps the Illampu, or the Illimani. The black 'cross' is the world-wide 'heaven-propper' symbol which expresses magical protection from cosmic dangers. This interpretation is borne out by the little disk 'lying on the cross' and 'kept away' by it from the quartered 'Earth' symbol below it. The yellow colour is always conventionally attributed to the evil 'puma star', the former Satellite, on the polychromous pottery of Tiahuanaco.

DIAGRAM 3

The 'Map of Ttahua-ntin-suyu'

classical Tiahuanaco style, nothing clumsy and groping and earthy; it is, rather, everywhere expressive of an advanced intellect, and full of a charm of its own and of considerable humour. It is a full-blown and completely stabilized style, for it shows neither development from naturalism nor decay into soulless clichéism. The former phenomenon is due to the fact that it is a transplantation from elsewhere, the latter to the fact of its dramatic extinction. It is a 'national' style, for it seems to be the only one applied in the Tiahuanaco culture area of that period.

All linear ornaments of the classic Tiahuanaco style always show a sovereign sureness of design. Especially the masterful mazes of the meanders captivate our admiration.

All figural ornaments show a supreme certainty of shape. They are very limited in number. The most important are: the puma, the condor, the toxodon, the fish, and the disk. (Cf. the List of Numerical Symbols, pp. 109-116.)

In spite of their severely 'stylized' form these figural elements are surprisingly expressive: the serene 'aquilinity' of the condors, the furtive 'felinity' of the pumas, the vacant 'piscinity' of the fishes, and the placid stupidity of the toxodons, are marvellous.

The figural ornaments show certain peculiar and significant mannerisms. The eyes of all beings depicted are always drawn disproportionately large, as if to 'point' at the value of sight and observation. Pumas and toxodons always have a disk-like 'nose'; the meaning of this determinative symbol will be explained later. All animal heads have a peculiar 'collar'. Big condor-heads are depicted with circular 'ears', and very big ones also with 'nostrils'. Other mannerisms will be referred to later.

We do not know the tools—chisels and gravers, chiefly—with which the hard andesite was worked to such perfection. For they seem to have cut and graved the stubborn material as if it was steatite. Even modern steel tools of average quality are quickly blunted by the fine, close texture of the stone. Possibly the Tiahuanacans knew of a secret process to harden bronze. The implements hitherto excavated are not hard enough; either they have depreciated in toughness and temper, or they are not identical with those which formed the rough blocks of andesite into their strange but exactly worked shapes. Besides, these tools are clumsy and would not have allowed the cutting of the sometimes almost filigree-like ornaments.

It is certain that the appearance of bronze tools in the culture-strata of Tiahuanaco coincided with the arrival of the new immigrants of superior race and high scientific and artistic accomplishments, who were responsible for the classic period. Copper had been known and used before, but the newcomers mined for tin. Evidences of prehistoric workings have recently been discovered in the Cordilleras about 90 miles from Tiahuanaco. The fact of the exceedingly great age of these workings is firmly established, for they were buried under a glacier and became exposed only a few years ago by the retreat of the ice.

At that time also, plenty of good timber must have been available in the Tiahuanaco Asylum for the building of ships, or barges, or sea-going rafts, as gigantic stone blocks and slabs weighing at times many tens of tons could not possibly have been transported over thirty or more miles of open sea in vessels similar to the clumsy and easily water-logged balsas, boats made of plaited rushes and reeds, in which the Indians go fishing on Lake Titicaca in our days.

Also for the unloading, lifting, and eventual placing *in situ* of the blocks, strong timber constructions would be necessary.

Some of the vessels of that time, though well built, must have suffered shipwreck within sight of the harbours of Tiahuanaco. For between the present shore of Lake Titicaca and the ruins of the prehistoric metropolis have been found several 'dumps' of roughly squared and half-worked stone. Their presence there is best explained by the theory that they represent the cargoes of transport vessels which had sunk in the waters of the Inter-Andean Sea of the Intermediate Level.

THE RISE OF A NEW CULTURE

It is not convincing to say, as some do, that these 'dumps' are *piedras cansadas*, 'tired stones'—stones, that is, which the transport workers got tired of shifting to a Tiahuanaco that never was a harbour city and was not contemporaneous with the Inter-Andean Sea of the Intermediate Strandline.

Tiahuanaco is not the only site of the Second Period of Culture found in the Altiplano of the Andes. Quite a number of settlements of a similar, or related, style have been discovered, though so far they have hardly been explored. Bolivia is not yet awake enough to take a profound and lasting interest in archaeological exploration, or, at any rate, to finance such work as handsomely as it deserves. For no very clear reason, the great Scientific Foundations have neglected those hidden-away sites hitherto. Yet a detailed survey especially of those areas of the Altiplano which were above the level of the Intermediate Inter-Andean Sea would bring about results which might well be astounding.

5

THE ENIGMA OF TIAHUANACO

———⇒◉⇐———

The remaining part of this book will be devoted chiefly to the discussion of the problems of the prehistoric city of Tiahuanaco, and to the Second Period of Culture, of which it is the outstanding example.

The ruin-field of Tiahuanaco lies on the railway line from La Paz, the capital of Bolivia, to Guaqui, the Bolivian harbour-town on Lake Titicaca, in the latitude of 16° 37′ S., and the longitude of 68° 41′ W.[17] The site covers a slight rise in a very long and extremely shallow valley, which is some six miles wide and bordered by low hills, the range of Achuta to the north, and the range of Quimsachata to the south. It is situated 12,596 feet above sea-level,[18] and ninety feet above the present level of Lake Titicaca. There are many unmistakable evidences that originally Tiahuanaco was a harbour-city; but the shore of the lake is now about 12½ miles away, so gently does the land slope. Near the ruin-field lies the Tiahuanaco of our days, a village of some 500 inhabitants, unimportant except for the fact that—together with other places in that region—it constitutes a repository of the loot taken in the course of the last centuries from the rich site of Prehistoric Tiahuanaco.

The actual name of the ancient city is forgotten. *Tiahuanaco* is the traditional local appellation which the Spaniards wormed, or squeezed, out of the Indians of this region. Re-interpreting an etymology suggested by the Hispano-Peruvian historian, 'Inca' Garcilaso de la Vega, its meaning may be something like 'the place where the guanaco, the wild llama, rests', which would describe the desolate wilderness in which

40

the astonished *conquistadores* found the surprising ruins. However, this interpretation somehow smacks strongly of popular etymology. But there is another explanation of the word Tiahuanaco which seems to have a more authentic ring. It must have been suggested shortly after the conquest that the meaning of the word was something like 'Divine Island', literally 'Divine Water Stone', i.e. 'Firm Land, kept by the Gods above Waters'. Anyhow, the Spanish Archbishop Taborga, who took considerable and sympathetic interest in the fast-crumbling culture of the conquered regions of South America, accepts this suggestion and renders it as 'the Country of the Omnipotent God which is situated above the Waters'. An appellation like that would be very apposite, and would, in fact, be borne out by a name which the Aymara gave to the site: *Taipi-ccala*, literally 'Centre Stone', or, more freely rendered, 'Stone Building in the Centre (*sc.*, of the World[19])'. Hence it is not improbable that the name 'Tiahuanaco' is as clear an echo of the forgotten original name of the great prehistoric city as it is possible to sound across a chasm of time which may be hundreds of thousands of years wide.[20]

There is one other derivation, which is too peculiar not to be mentioned. According to the *Enciclopedia Universal* the Quechua words *Tiya-huanuk* mean 'failing light', and are said to refer to the worship of the god Ka-Ata-Killa, the 'Decaying Moon', to whom human sacrifices were offered to save him from death. In the light of our Theory of the disintegration of satellites this explanation of Tiahuanaco as the 'City of the time of the doomed Satellite' would be very significant.[21]

The ruin-field of Tiahuanaco has at all times been a problem to the investigator. It was a ruin-field (though an incomparably richer one) in the time of the Incas, who not only appear to have taken no interest in it, but actually seem to have avoided it. Though they built a considerable number of settlements, including two of their most sacred shrines, in the Inter-Andean Altiplano, they do not seem to have used Tiahuanaco

41

even as a source of building material. The site was probably taboo. The Spanish chroniclers could gather practically no traditions regarding the builders of the astonishing structures of Tiahuanaco, but this is not to be wondered at since the *conquistadores* had killed off practically everybody of rank in that region in their first onset, and the inquisitor-missionaries who had come in their wake had dealt equally efficiently, if less violently, with any who obdurately treasured ancient lore and knowledge.

However, as happens in all similar cases at all times, a certain amount of traditional material must have been driven 'underground' and handed on secretly in the form of 'Myths'. But the Indians of the Tiahuanaco Region are not communicative, and only little is known about their folklore and cosmology. All that has hitherto been coaxed out of those stolid men is that 'the great ruined city was built prior to a terrible cataclysm, which they call *Chamak-Pacha*, the Age of Darkness, and that formerly most of what is now the wide Inter-Andean Plain was a great sea rich in big fish; eventually the builders of the city had been destroyed by a flood'. Some of these Indians call themselves 'Urus', which means something like 'Men of the Light'. They hint that they had lived in the Bolivian highlands already before the Age of Darkness, and that they remember the time 'when the Sun appeared' (i.e. became visible again in the heavens after that cataclysm).

The 'Christianity' of the Indians of the Titicaca region is, luckily, not more than skin-deep: an ethnographer who would be able to win their confidence, might procure much interesting and valuable material there.

History—whether recorded or traditional—being silent, any authoritative statement as to the age, and as to the reason for the position and form, of the prehistoric city can only come from the ruins themselves. And they impress upon the beholder in a multitude of ways the fact that they are really exceedingly ancient.

The measurements of some of the buildings of Tiahuanaco

are astounding. The 'fortress' of Akapana measures about
650 by 600 feet (roughly equal to the area of the Tower of
London, inside the Moat); the outer walls of the great Sun
Temple of Kalasasaya measure about 440 by 390 feet
(roughly equal to the area of Trafalgar Square); those of the
'Palace of the Black-White-and-Red Stairs', also called the
'Palace of the Sarcophagi', measure 220 by 180 feet (roughly
equal to the area of Leicester Square). All the great buildings
of Tiahuanaco, except small parts of them, were open to the
sky, and evidently gathering-places for vast multitudes who
met for political, religious, and social purposes. The more one
contemplates these and other remains of the Tiahuanaco culture the more one gets the vivid impression that they were the
result of a co-operative rather than a competitive civilization, a
real democracy, free from any oppression, guided by a clear,
definite, and urgent culture-will. In size they are comparable
to the arenas, amphitheatres, and stadia of the Old World.
Edifices of such lay-out seem singularly out of place in a
region with a cold, raw climate. Indeed, the more we study
them the more we are convinced that at the time when they
were built the climate in the Andean Altiplano must have been
tropical.

6

THE MIGHTIEST STONES IN THE WORLD

———————◦◦◦———————

The style of the Second Culture Period of Tiahuanaco is 'megalithic'—but not 'cyclopean'. Though its history of evolution is quite unknown, it does not seem to be descended directly from cromlech-like or dolmen-like primitive stone pilings, those first steps of prehistoric man towards architecture. The tendency of all architecture everywhere in the world was, and is, to reduce the size of the building elements—

DIAGRAM 4

A typical example of the intricate shape of some of the building elements of the 'classical' Tiahuanaco period. This monolith, which measures about 9' 3" by 5' 2" by 2' 11" and weighs more than 8 tons, is cut on all 'six' surfaces. Evidently the shallow sockets were intended to receive matching projections of other building elements. What shape these latter may have had is utterly incomprehensible. The exact function which the block shown may have had as part of an edifice is equally unfathomable. With some architect friends the writer has toyed for weeks with a model of this block and its likely extensions, but it was impossible to find a satisfactory approach. All that can be said is that the form of the glass-hard andesite block is evidently purposeful and that the intricate mortising together must have given immense powers of resistance to earthquake. shocks to the building it was (intended to be) part of.

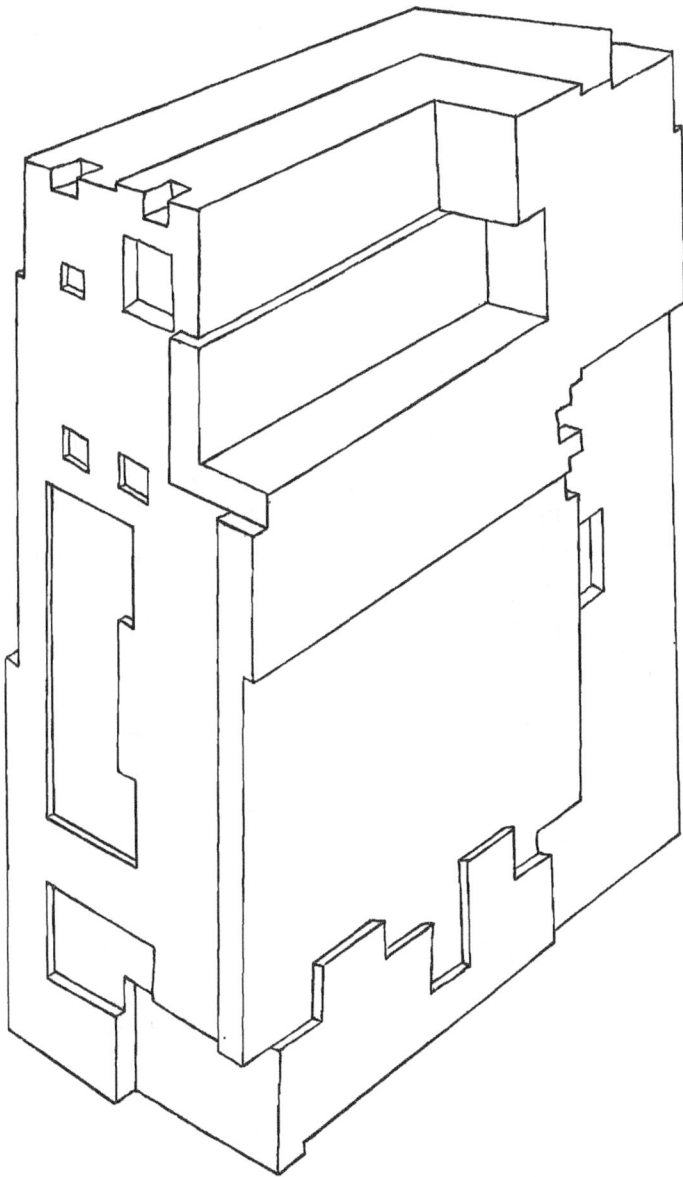

DIAGRAM 4

45

bricks, squared stone blocks, slabs, etc.—and to attain the desired artistic or utilitarian effect by the artful arrangement of normalized elements. A building is thus reared upon foundation walls; a door, in its simplest form, is formed of two jambs and a lintel; a wall is built of individual blocks; and a niche in that wall, or a cornice, is formed by setting these blocks back from, or letting them project over, the general wall surface.

As far as we can judge from the remains of the First Culture Period of Tiahuanaco their style of building was of that nature. But the architects of Tiahuanaco the Second followed other paths. Instead of reducing the size of the building elements, and normalizing them, they seem to have increased their size, and fashioned almost each one of them individually. The form of many of these major building elements is frequently most fantastic and utterly puzzling. (Cf. Diagram 4 on p. 45.) They used smaller and more normalized building elements too, of course—nearly all the houses, churches, etc., in the neighbourhood of Tiahuanaco have been built of this looted material. But for some reason or other, the Tiahuanaco architects gave up constructing their most important edifices out of small elements. Instead of building a piece of wall out of scores, or hundreds, of bonded, etc., smaller elements, they chiselled that portion of wall in one piece out of a huge block. Niches, cornices, or projecting ornaments, have thus been produced by the sculptor, and not by the builder's arrangement of his elements. (Cf. Diagram 13 on p. 87.) The gateways of the public buildings of Tiahuanaco seem by preference to have been monolithic; some of them, however, were trilithic, that is, consisting of two uprights and one lintel (cf. Diagram 7 on p. 49); the construction of polylithic doorways (cf. Diagram 8 on p. 49) composed of a number of small elements seems to have been avoided by the Tiahuanacans. Important parts of edifices are based upon enormous foundation slabs. These huge and complicated elements were united by means of cramps, or they were mortised, or keyed, together.

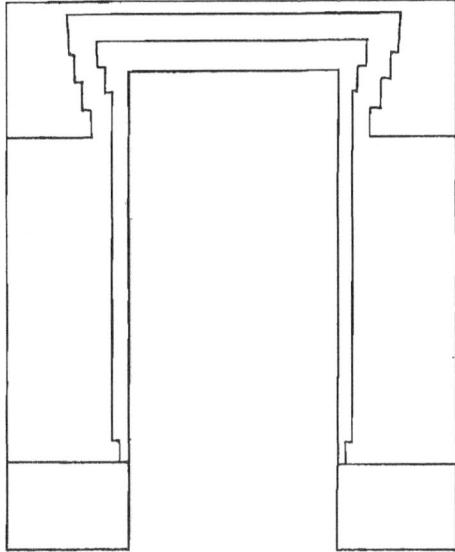

DIAGRAM 5   DIAGRAM 6

DIAGRAM 5

Completely monolithic gateway, lintel, jambs, *and threshold* cut out of one slab (in this instance of a hard red sandstone). This is the only example of a framelike gateway found at Tiahuanaco.

DIAGRAM 6

Monolithic gateway cut out of one slab of andesite. Was at one time part of the Sun Temple of Kalasasaya. Its front shows a much obliterated 'continuation' of the 'meander-line' of the Calendar. It is remarkable that it has remained unbroken, seeing that its 'lintel' is only a little over a foot thick. It has been put to use as the entrance to a small, now disused, cemetery of the present village of Tiahuanaco.

The famous sculptured 'Calendar Gate' (cf. Diagrams 12 and 13, on p. 87), for instance, which was found in the precincts of the Sun Temple of Kalasasaya, is about 10 ft. high by $12\frac{1}{2}$ ft. wide, and 18 in. thick. Its weight is about ten tons. But many other structural parts of this and other edifices are incomparably bigger; many of the andesite blocks weigh more than sixty tons, while the weight of some of the sand-stone blocks has been estimated to exceed a hundred tons. In their rough, unworked state they must have been very much heavier still.

Nowhere on Earth do we find anything comparable to or reminiscent of this architecture. This style of megalithic architecture is so original and unique that it has no name—apart from that of its site, Tiahuanaco.

What suggested, or what dictated, this way of building? Considering the maturity and planfulness of everything found on the ruin-field of Tiahuanaco, it is absolutely certain that

---

DIAGRAM 7

Trilithic Gateway, consisting of two 'jambs' and a 'lintel'. (Only the left 'jamb', constituting also an appreciable portion of 'wall', has been found. Its fellow and the 'lintel'—which may have been shorter or longer—have here been tentatively added. The find proves that this method of construction was known, though it was evidently only little used.)

DIAGRAM 8

Polylithic Gateway constructed by the builder of the 'Inka Tambo' (Inn of the Inca), or 'Ccala-uta' (Stone House), an otherwise humble homestead near Tiahuanaco, out of 34 individual smaller pieces of material looted from Puma Punku, which originally must have been destined for quite different purposes. This method of building doorways was avoided by the Tiahuanacans.[21a]

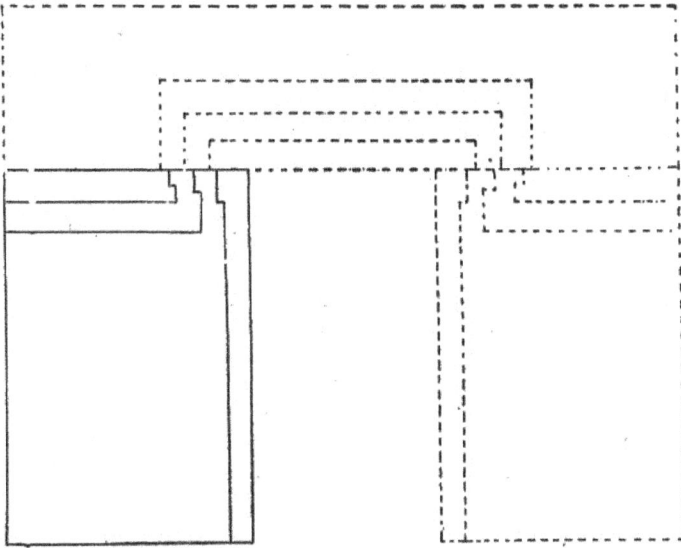

DIAGRAM 7

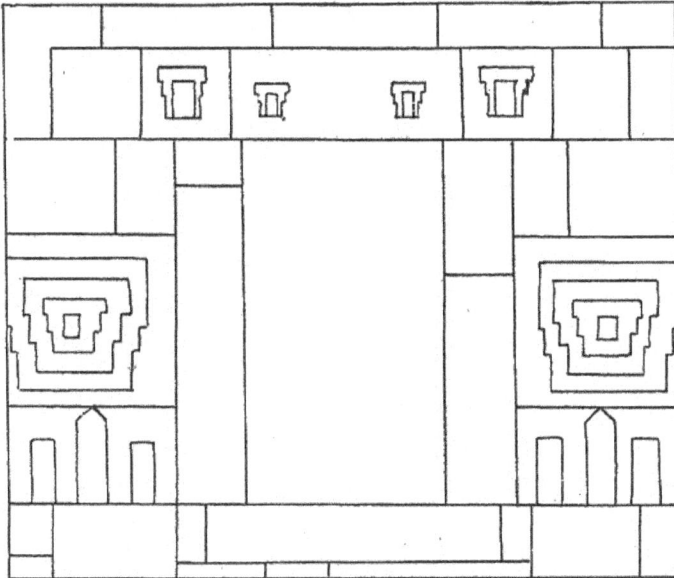

DIAGRAM 8

49

the peculiar method of building employed there was not due to the whim of a tyrant in architecture, or to the incapability of the builders to think in terms of small elements, artfully arranged. It must have been dictated by considerations based upon exigencies of nature which were imperative at the time when these buildings were reared, and it must have been developed intentionally to meet those exigencies.

What were those exigencies? The ruins themselves speak in evidence. Though the builders have used bronze cramps, at times of very elaborate shape, most of the masonry of Tiahuanaco, and other megalithic sites in this region, was kept in place by gravitation, and also—and perhaps chiefly—by that strong adhesion which comes into play when absolutely plane and highly polished surfaces of heavy blocks touch. Mortar has never been used anywhere apparently, during this 'classical period', but many of the building elements are joined together by carefully matched tenons and mortises, sometimes even multiple ones. The walls of edifices thus built would be both extremely 'solid', and yet exceedingly 'elastic', and hence practically impervious to earthquake shocks. Indeed, the closer we investigate into the architectural remains of the Second Period of Tiahuanaco, the more we gain the impression that at the time when the buildings were planned the world was somehow different—strangely different. The surmise that the builders of Tiahuanaco constructed their edifices with a definite intention to make them quake- and tremor-proof is strengthened by the other peculiarities of the buildings which all fit into the same picture: Edifices were built of a few big elements, not of many small ones; there were no two or more storied buildings; some edifices were built *into* the ground; the chief parts of many of the buildings were reared on exceedingly heavy foundation slabs, whose inert weight alone was a certain protection from wave-like heavings of the ground; and doors and windows were hewn in one piece out of blocks, or slabs, of andesite, and not composed of sills, jambs, and lintels. Buildings thus reared will

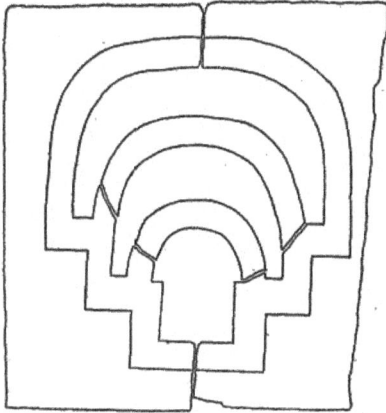

DIAGRAM 9

Monolithic window of unique design, found in the Sun Temple of Kalasasaya. This magnificent specimen of masterful stone-carving has been cut out of a slab of andesite measuring about 32 by 32 by 8 inches.[21b]

not collapse into heaps of rubble even under very severe shocks, and, if made of one piece, those points of weakness in the walls, the doors and windows, will not give way and trap the inmates.

Thus, then, the Sacred City of Tiahuanaco was built. (Cf. Diagram 10, p. 53.) The great Sun Temple of Kalasasaya,[22] with its monumental eastern stairway and its marvellous Calendar Gate, was erected. A small hill, which seems to have been a stronghold already of the First Period, was artificially enlarged and shaped into the vast, many-bastioned, three-stepped 'ziqqurat'-like fortress of Akapana[23] whose top-platform had an area of eight acres, and featured, amongst other things, a large pond or basin. The splendid 'Palace of the Black-White-and-Red Stairs', also called the 'Palace of the Sarcophagi', an edifice of unknown use, was built. Also peculiar, small, subterranean, 'shelter'-like, earthquake-proof one room 'dwellings' were constructed of finely worked, heavy slabs which were intricately keyed and mortised together. The 'Canal' which surrounds all these remains, and separated them from other parts of the ancient city which have not yet been explored, was dug. About three-quarters of a mile to the south-west of Tiahuanaco proper, the extensive edifice named 'Puma Punku' rose.[24] The rectangular harbour basin, or dock, which is situated a little over a hundred yards north of the Temple of Kalasasaya, and the two docks immediately before Puma Punku, were made. Some distance south-east of Puma Punku rose Huila Pukara, the 'Red, or Coloured, Fortress', a building comparable to Akapana, but smaller. The little-explored group of ruins called Chuqui-Pacha, near Tiahuanaco, may have been a military settlement, at least judging from its name which means 'Place of Lances'. And the extensive prehistoric settlement underlying the present-day village of Tiahuanaco, probably the Secular City, was laid out.

The 'dwellings' mentioned in the preceding paragraph, which are situated at the north-western corner of the Sun Temple of Kalasasaya, are the only edifices hitherto discovered which may be said to give us any direct indication as to how the Tiahuanacans, or at least some of them, were housed. On an average the 'dwellings' measure only 4 ft. 8 in. long by 4 ft. 4 in. wide and 4 ft. 6 in. high. The thick, well squared slabs with which they were covered were level with the ground. Access was gained through a square opening in one corner of this roof, or ceiling, from which steep, short, narrow steps led down to the stone floor. In one corner of the tiny room was a raised hearth; the smoke escaped through a circular hole above this fireplace. The size of the room allowed the inmate—there can hardly have been more than one—only to squat, and he could only have slept in the posture in which Indians of this region sleep in our days: wrapped in a poncho, with knees drawn up towards the chin and head lying on the arms which rested on the knees.—Whether these dwellings were typical for the Tiahuanacans is not known. The site of the prehistoric 'profane' settlement is now covered by the sprawling present-day village of Tiahuanaco which makes digging a difficult and delicate procedure. The close proximity of the underground 'dwellings' to the Temple of Kalasasaya gives support to the idea that they may have been 'cells' of anchorites, or of sacerdotal or janitorial staff attached to this chief sacred edifice of Tiahuanaco.

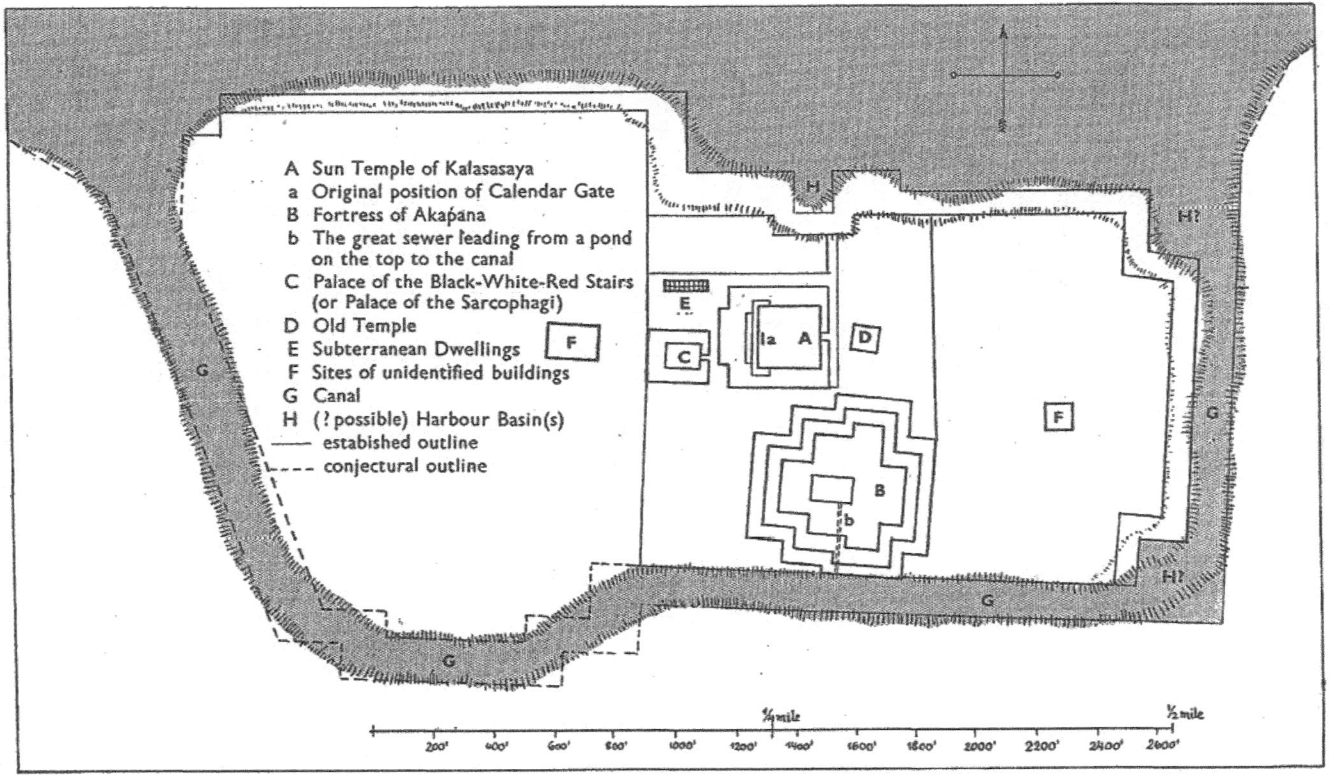

A Sun Temple of Kalasasaya
a Original position of Calendar Gate
B Fortress of Akápana
b The great sewer leading from a pond on the top to the canal
C Palace of the Black-White-Red Stairs (or Palace of the Sarcophagi)
D Old Temple
E Subterranean Dwellings
F Sites of unidentified buildings
G Canal
H (? possible) Harbour Basin(s)
— established outline
--- conjectural outline

½ mile

¼ mile

200' 400' 600' 800' 1000' 1200' 1400' 1600' 1800' 2000' 2200' 2400' 2600'

DIAGRAM 10: THE 'SACRED CITY' OF TIAHUANACO (after Posnansky)

The general outline of the 'island' is proved by the 'canal'; the special outline here attributed to it is partly based on the remains of 'quay walls' and partly upon the fact that the Tiahuanacans tended to give a geometrical 'escalinated' form not only to their buildings but also to the sites containing them.

53

THE MIGHTIEST STONES IN THE WORLD

Nowadays the site of Tiahuanaco shows little more than a few megalithic blocks of worked stone. Before the Conquest, however, the area of the great prehistoric city must have offered a wonderful appearance. But for centuries the European settlers there have used the site for a quarry, plundering it ruthlessly to build most of the houses, churches, and bridges of Tiahuanaco, La Paz, Laja, and other towns. Stones whose prominent ornamentation made them unfit for immediate use were roughly chipped into a more serviceable shape; others which showed the masterful meanders and complicated trapeziums of the classic Tiahuanaco style were defaced before being used to obtain smoother surfaces. This vandalism was continued in more recent times when speculating contractors, out for quick returns, had the region scoured for most of what remained of any ready-dressed material to build railway embankments and roads. Nor has the craving for worked stones abated in our days. Any block or slab of convenient weight uncovered by an excavator is stolen overnight. An exceedingly interesting and well-made drainage construction on the southern slope of the 'fortress' of Akapana was thus destroyed by local vandals, luckily only after it had been photographed. The black, white, and red stones of a beautiful flight of steps in the 'Palace of the Sarcophagi' were likewise stolen soon after they were excavated, and only a photograph tells of their original location now. Hence the site of Tiahuanaco now contains only those blocks which offered, and still offer, passive resistance to removal by being too heavy or by being out of sight, covered with a good layer of soil.

In spite of all this discouraging interference, modern archaeologists, pre-eminently that great Americanist and greatest Tiahuanacologist, Professor Arthur Posnansky, of La Paz, have made the robbed and mangled site one of surpassing interest and importance. They traced the ground-plans of the edifices mentioned, surveyed the surrounding country, and secured a number of extremely valuable objects for the Museums.

Yet infinitely more remains to be done. For the hitherto hardly explored lower strata of wide regions yield pottery, implements, sculptures, and tooled stones, as well as considerable and interesting layers of the scattered broken bones of men and of (since extinct) animals. Up till now only test-pits have been sunk here and there on the site of Tiahuanaco, down to the 'virgin' soil, but no large-scale modern excavations have ever been attempted yet.

7

THE PROBLEMS OF THE SLANTING
STRANDLINE

Perhaps the greatest and most puzzling discovery which was made in connexion with Tiahuanaco was that at the time when the buildings of the so-called 'Second Period' were erected, the prehistoric metropolis was not a city sprawling upon a gentle rise in a wide valley, but one situated on the shore in a sheltered bight of a sort of peninsula. For Tiahuanaco was a harbour-city, the remains of whose quay walls are still distinctly discernible, while a number of docklike harbour-basins and a canal can also be traced. This 'canal' actually made Tiahuanaco proper—i.e. the 'sacred city' with the vast monumental edifices—into a small island, measuring about 1100 by 500 yards. (Cf. the plan, Diagram 10, on p. 53). Whether this was done for purposes of prestige or defence, or whether the canal was constructed for communication and trade, cannot be decided now.[25]

The existence of the harbour-basins and the canal would lead us to think that at the time when the ancient city of Tiahuanaco was in its prime and glory, the level of Lake Titicaca was about 90 feet higher than it is now. On that assumption, the shallow sluggish Desaguadero would then have been not a river, but a deep, winding 'strait', some 8 to 30 miles wide, and some 180 miles long, which led to a vast sheet of water covering all the region of Lake Poöpo, Lake Coipasa, and the salt-deserts of Coipasa and Uyuni.

But this apparently inevitable conclusion is found to be impossible on looking closer into the matter. For the sheet of water on whose shore Tiahuanaco was situated has left a very distinct trace of its former presence: a strandline.

And this strandline tells another, and a very strange, story.

It has been carefully surveyed for a length of about 375 miles. And then it was established—that it is not 'straight'. It was found that the Inter-Andean Sea of the Intermediate Level was not merely a Lake Titicaca of higher level extending far to the south, but that its level showed a slant of a most peculiar character in relation to the present ocean-level, or, which amounts to the same, relative to the present level of Lake Titicaca. (Cf. Diagram 11, facing p. 58.)

The level of the Inter-Andean Sea revealed by the ancient intermediate strandline was higher to the north of Tiahuanaco and lower to the south.

The actuality of this peculiarity cannot be doubted, for it was established independently by different persons at different times, using different methods of surveying.

The northernmost point at which the former strandline of the Inter-Andean Sea of the Intermediate Level has been surveyed is on the mountain-slopes near Sillustani, to the west of Lake Umayo[26] in the Peruvian Department of Puno. There the former littoral is about 295 feet above the present level of Lake Titicaca, whose surface is 12,506 feet above sea-level. At Tiahuanaco, at the southern end of Lake Titicaca, the same strandline is 90 feet above the level of that great sheet of water, and 4 feet below the coping-stones of the parapets of the long-dry harbours and docks and canals of that mysterious metropolis. The ancient strandline and the ruined prehistoric city are linked beyond any doubt. The height of the strandline relative to the ocean-level decreases the further south we go. At the northern end of Lake Poöpo, on the mountain-slopes south of Oruro, it is 12,232 feet above sea-level, or 181 feet above the level of Lake Poöpo, or 274 feet below the level of Lake Titicaca, or 364 feet below the level of the same ancient strandline in the latitude of Tiahuanaco. Still further to the south, it is discernible just a few feet above the level of Lake

DIAGRAM 11

This Ideal longitudinal section through the Bolivian Altiplano (along different meridians between 69°30′ and 67°30′ W to obtain a clearer diagram) shows the three levels of the former Inter-Andean Sea, with relation to Tiahuanaco. To show up distinctly the slant of the levels as revealed by the ancient strandlines all heights have been exaggerated 500 times. (Cf. also the Map of the Bolivian Altiplano, facing page 14, especially for the key to the colouring.)

Present levels of the Lakes in the Meseta: Titicaca 12506 ft., Poöpo 12051 ft., Coipasa 12031 ft. above sea-level.

..........Inter-Andean Sea of the Lowest Level (conjectural): southern shore slightly lower than Lake Titicaca, northern shore not determined.

--------- Inter-Andean Sea of the Intermediate Level: strandline dipping from about 12800 ft. in the north (12596 ft. at Tiahuanaco) to about 12000 ft. in the south.

-·-·-·-·-· Inter-Andean Sea of the Highest Level: strandline dipping from about 13550 ft. in the north (13266 ft. in the latitude of Tiahuanaco) to about 12500 ft. in the south.

La Paz Gap about 12800 ft., Uyuni Gap about 12800 ft., Ascotan Gap about 12400 ft. above sea level.

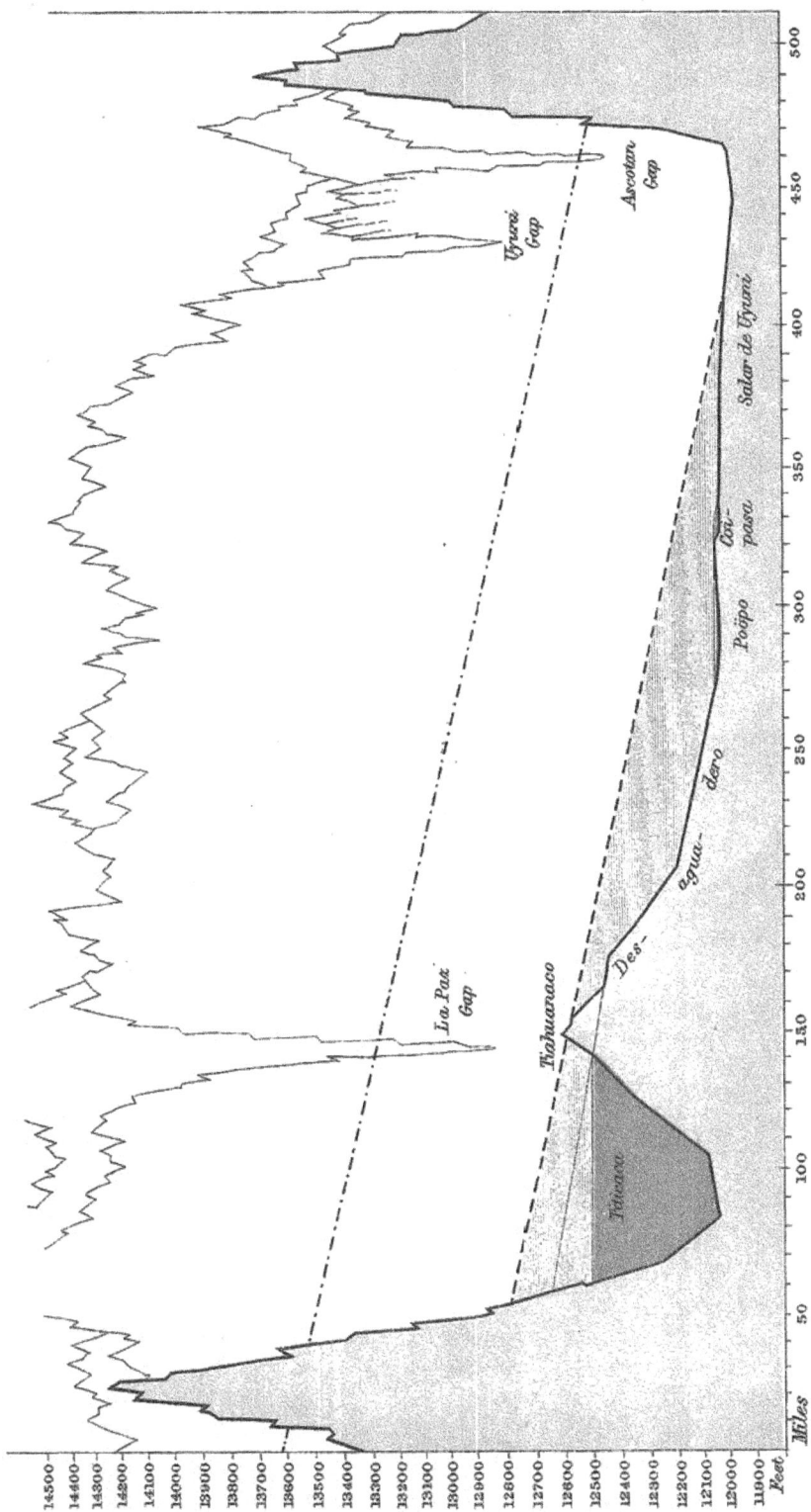

IDEAL LONGITUDINAL SECTION
THROUGH THE BOLIVIAN ALTIPLANO (ANDINIAN REFUGE)

Coipasa. It becomes lost in the Salt Desert of Uyuni, some 12,000 feet above sea-level.

From Sillustani to beyond Lake Coipasa, a distance of about 375 miles, the strandline dips about 800 feet. A peculiarity of this dip is that it seems to be progressive. In the first quarter of the distance it is only about a foot and a quarter per mile, while in the last fourth it increases to more than two feet per mile. This phenomenon is not without significance and yields a prop for the theory that the waters were controlled by the gravitation of a close satellite.

The strandline of the Inter-Andean Sea of the Intermediate Level is very distinct. It consists not only of notches cut into the rock by the prolonged action of shore-waves, and of fan-like delta-deposits of mud and gravel, which former streams dropped on meeting the ancient water's edge, but chiefly of conspicuous deposits of white lime, of a thickness of many feet, upon the red sandstone, or brown porphyry and amorphous slate, or grey granite and andesite. This white streak, which is drawn along the slopes of the mountain-chains surrounding the Altiplano, and visible on the islands in Lake Titicaca like a chalk-line, is the residue of certain calcareous algae, chiefly of *alga characea*. This lowly organized plant, which contains about 80 per cent. of lime, is still found growing in certain shallow shore-parts of Lake Titicaca. It only thrives in slightly muddy water down to a depth not exceeding three feet.

The phenomenon of the slanting strandline is usually said to have come about through an 'unbalanced rise' of South America out of the waters of the Ocean. The forces, it is said, which lifted up the continent, acted more strongly in the north than in the south: hence the level of the former Inter-Andean Sea is not parallel to that of Lake Titicaca or the Ocean. Judging from palaeontological evidence, this uplift is said to have been quite 'recent', geologically speaking. It must, in fact, have happened towards the end of the Tertiary Age. Then, quite suddenly, literally with a jerk, the Andes must have been raised up more than 12,300 feet on an average.

THE PROBLEMS OF THE SLANTING STRANDLINE

The explanation given by Hoerbiger's Cosmological Theory regarding the Earth's Satellites seems to be much more likely than that of orthodox science. It would certainly explain better the slightly bulging slant of the Intermediary Strandline, for the powerful pull of the former Satellite would cause the level of all waters of the Earth to be highest in the zone where its orbital plane intersected the terrestrial globe, and lower to the south and north of this zone. Besides, Hoerbiger's Cosmological Theory will be found to give a very plausible reason why there is an Inter-Andean Sea of a still higher strandline (cf. pp. 68 f.), and it will be found to suggest solutions for all the biological, palaeontological, climatological, archaeological, and other enigmas, which make the Tiahuanaco problem so puzzling.

8

THE SELECTION OF THE SITE

One of the greatest enigmas, for which orthodox science has not been able hitherto to give a satisfactory explanation, is the choice of the locality in which Tiahuanaco is situated. The problem is really a two-fold one: Why was Tiahuanaco built in that highly elevated region? And why was its site just in that spot? The former question is less difficult to answer than the latter.

The present environs of the prehistoric metropolis are disappointing, not to say forbidding. There seems to be practically nothing which might help to explain the flowering of so strangely high a culture in that region. The ruins of the great city are surrounded by a desolate waste with hardly any vegetation except rough grass; where no cereals grow except barley, and even this frequently fails to ripen; wheat is poor; maize is dwarfish and scant, the cobs hardly ever exceeding an inch in length; potatoes[27] and some other tubers are the only food which can be grown locally to any advantage. The hills which frame Tiahuanaco are grim and sterile, and yield no timber. Such is the flora, while the fauna is similarly scarce and stunted. The biggest animal native to the region is the nimble, but weak, llama. The fishes of Lake Titicaca are not numerous, and small—evidently degenerated. At the great height at which Tiahuanaco is situated life for man and beast is only possible with an effort, and the unremitting struggle against cold, thin air, and poor food, is exhausting.

The magnitude and grandeur of the vast edifices of Tiahuanaco and the other sites, however, impress upon us the fact that they were built by ably-led armies of workers for multitudes of men who were able to appreciate them, and, indeed, probably expected them to be just so and not otherwise. The huge, carefully thought out, and beautifully worked elements of which the edifices of Tiahuanaco were reared do not give the impression that their raw material was brought from afar, hewn into shape, and piled into buildings, by masses of slaves, meagrely fed on imported provisions, toiling with primitive tools, panting in the thin air. No—the more one considers all these factors, the more one is convinced that, at the time when the enigmatic city was built, very different climatic and other conditions obtained in this part of the world, nay, that the whole world then showed quite another face.

Here Hoerbiger's Theory is helpful. At the time when the predecessor of our present Moon had approached so close through cosmic reasons that it swung round the Earth about three times in two days, the waters of the oceans had been drawn into the tropical zone and held there in a great tidal belt, the 'girdle-tide'. The axis, or central line, of this watering-ring coincided with the line where the orbital plane of the Satellite intersected the terrestrial globe. The atmosphere had been drawn into a similar, though somewhat less pronounced tide-ring, making the 'air-blanket' in the polar regions and higher latitudes very threadbare. The girdle-tide was continuous in its central part. In its more northern and southern zones land areas existed as islands, or small continents, the tropical 'life asylums' or 'island refuges'. Still further north and south were situated the northern and southern 'zone refuges', between the shores of the great tidal ring and the fringes of the great ice-caps which then extended from the poles far into what we now call the 'temperate zones'. (Cf. Diagram 2 on p. 23.)

All surviving life withdrew to these zone refuges and to the islands set in the girdle-tide. In the northern and southern zone refuges life was very hard; culture was of necessity rather low as the tribes never became sessile in the vast, cold, tundra-like expanses. The tropical life asylums, on the other hand, were warm island-paradises.

These island refuges were the densely crowded, chief seats of the human and animal life of that time, and of plant life too. The numerous practically or entirely sessile tribes were not only able to carry on agriculture and horticulture, but also to cultivate the arts and practise the sciences.

At the time when Tiahuanaco was built, 'Andinia' was one of those tropical island refuges.

This assertion is amply borne out by biological, palaeontological, and archaeological evidence. Among the biological proofs may be mentioned the occurrence of certain plants (stunted ferns, etc.) which seem to be out of place in so elevated a region, and the presence of hippocampi (sea-horses) in the cold waters of Lake Titicaca. Palaeontological proofs are, for example, the charred remains of a former rich vegetation which have been discovered under a layer of volcanic ashes, and the remains of giant turtles and other warmth-loving animals in the alluvial strata of the Altiplano. Archaeological proofs are, among others, the vast public buildings and temples which are open to the sky, and the sculptural representation of certain animals, such as the flying fish and certain crustaceans, batrachidae, and mussels. Furthermore, the fact that fish-heads are used as a very frequent ornament reveals that the Sea of Tiahuanaco must have been teeming with fishes as only tropical waters are in our time.

So much for the question why Tiahuanaco was built in that 'highly elevated, practically barren' territory. It was really built 'at sea-level', that is, at the then level of the girdle-tide in that latitude.

The question why Tiahuanaco was built just at that spot does not allow of so ready an answer. The most likely incentive was probably that, for some reason or other, the site was considered 'sacred'. The Tiahuanaco of the First Period may well have been a politico-religious centre which had enjoyed far-reaching reputation in all Andinia—its 'Mecca', or its 'Rome'. The 'Old

Temple' of the First Period seems to have been a sort of regional ancestral shrine, if we interpret correctly the rows of sculptured heads set in its interior walls. Moreover, it had housed the monolithic statue, of gigantic dimensions, of a great deity, perhaps the supreme divine being of that region (cf. also Note 81). These facts, and the consideration that the great inundation catastrophe which brought about the end of the First Culture Period, though it apparently wrecked the Old Temple, did not submerge its site, may have caused the carriers of the Culture of the Second Period, who were evidently well used to a littoral or maritime life, to select just this spot as the site of their sacred capital.

For the feeding of the multitudes who populated Tiahuanaco and all the territory within its sacred and secular sway, all likely mountain-slopes of the Andinian Refuge had been laid out into agricultural terraces, called 'andenes' (Spanish for 'shelves'), or 'pata-pata' (Aymara for 'earth embankments'). The remains of these ancient agricultural terraces are never observed lower than about 13,000 feet above sea-level, for all these parts of the Meseta were then covered with water. Their upper limit is unknown; they probably were laid out up to the tops of even very high mountains—which then, of course, were some 12,000 feet 'lower'. On the mighty Illimani, for instance, which towers to over 21,000 feet, the terraces may be traced up to a height of about 18,400 feet, the present line of the eternal snow. Most of the mountain-sides in the neighbourhood of Lake Titicaca and other high-lying parts of Bolivia and Peru show more or less distinctly the remains of the low walls of hewn stone or rubble, by means of which the people of that time tried to utilize every square foot of the steep slopes. These most extensive agricultural terraces, on which nothing now grows, or has been known to grow since white men first saw them, must once have produced enough food for a population of many hundreds of thousands, perhaps even a few millions. Travellers often wonder at the presence of

the andenes in the thin air of those bleak and barren altitudes
where sustained hard work is impossible. Now, viewed from
the angle of Hoerbiger's Cosmological Theory, it appears
likely that they were built when a tropical climate prevailed
in the Andinian Life Asylum, and when a rich sub-tropical
vegetation covered even the highest elevations of that territory.

At the time of the Inter-Andean Sea of the Intermediate
Level, the Sea of Tiahuanaco, there was very little flat
land available, as the vast stretches of the present Meseta, or
Tableland, were under water. Hence the utilization of every
square foot of soil by terracing all mountain slopes into serviceable 'pata-pata' or 'andenes' was imperative. This made
so strong an impression upon the inhabitants of the Tiahuanaco Asylum that they chose the 'step-motif' as the most apposite symbol for expressing 'Earth' or 'World', and even for
what the Earth stood for—'Salvation' or 'Life':

They also used it in a profusion of forms for the ornamentation of their architecture, pottery, etc. The ground plan of
their temples also shows the 'step-motif'.

These extremely high agricultural terraces—traces of
which, by the way, are also to be met with in some of the
highest parts of Abyssinia, that other great Life Asylum in the
girdletide[28]—tell us plainly of a time when life in the lower,
flatter parts of the region was impossible, because they were
covered with water. The builders of these aids for intensive
agriculture in a terrain too steeply sloped to be easily worked
and economically exploited, erected them there because they
were forced to make the most of the last precious areas of good
land left to them by the inexorable cosmic powers. To stress it
once more: these andenes were built during the last stages of
the age of the girdle-tide, the great water-ring which was piled
higher and higher in equatorial and tropical latitudes by the
more and more closely approaching predecessor of our present

Moon. At no other time was there any reason or necessity to spend so much time and labour on their building. Besides, probably never since those far-off days when multitudes of fugitives from the encroaching girdle-tide crowded the Andinian Asylum has there been a sufficiency of labour in those regions to till these terraces. Nor would their working have been profitable under any but tropical or sub-tropical conditions.

The idea of a tropical girdle-tide caused by the gravitational pull of a former Satellite not only helps to resolve all the difficulties connected with Tiahuanaco and the neighbouring cultural remains, but also elucidates the other problems of the highest Andes, especially those attached to the utterly puzzling tightly-packed small settlements which here and there are perched, eyrie-like, upon improbable cliffs at impossible heights. The idea, which somehow has found credence among archaeologists, is that they were built by crazy architects bent upon performing impracticable tricks with difficult materials on unlikely sites, commissioned by maniacs for security and loneliness, and inhabited by people desirous of showing that they could live upon the produce of a few tiny andenes, while the builders scorned much more favourable sites situated only a little below the steep mountain-jags, and the agriculturists despised any available level ground in the valley-bottoms at the foot of their step-gardens. It was only because those much more likely regions were covered by the waters of the girdle-tide that they were not chosen. For Man always tends to take life as easily as possible—it is hard enough even then!

There is, for instance, the 'fortress' of Ollantay-Parubo, in the Urubamba Valley in Peru, impregnable because of its position, being perched upon a tiny plateau of some 13,000 feet above sea-level, in an uninhabitable region of precipices, chasms, and gorges, and indestructible because of its construction, being mostly built of megalithic, smoothly polished blocks of red porphyry. The material must have been brought from a considerable distance in a terrain which even modern transport technicians would shun to tackle—down steep slopes, across swift and turbulent rivers, and up precipitous rock-faces which hardly allow a foothold. But if water-transport across a fiord-like arm of a sea is supposed, this difficulty is removed and the choice of the site loses all its mystery.

Then, to mention another instance, there is the 'monastery' of Ollantay-Tambo, with its marvellous solar equinox observatory, the *inti-huatana*, whose position and construction are still bolder. The sun-worshipping 'monks' must have been first-class mountaineers to manage, as must certainly have been necessary sometimes, the ascent of, and descent from, the precipitous rocks of their retreat. If we picture them to have travelled to and from their settlements, and to have transported their materials there, by means of boats or rafts, sailing upon quiet fiords of the great girdle-tide, we get probably a much better and truer conception of the strange world which archaeology has proved to have existed in the 'thin air' of the 'highest' Andes in the remote past.

When the Incas eventually occupied these regions they utilized some of these surprising sites of a long-dead culture for a time, for strategic purposes, to house their garrisons. They reared upon the mighty foundations their own architecturally and technically differently conceived edifices. Their small-stone walls soon crumbled when the Inca empire crashed. Massily, however, still stand the ancient megalithic substructures, ready in their mortised strength to view serenely the further march-past of the millennia.

The reports of the investigators of these eyrie-like settlements contain no mention of strandlines, but they may be very inconspicuous and will reveal their presence only when looked for—as they certainly will be after this suggestion of ours.

In the neighbourhood of Cuzco certain observations of the former littorals have already been made, and the sheet of water which once filled the Cuzco Basin has even been given a name: 'Lake Morkill', after the geographer who first drew attention to its former presence.

9

THE END OF A WORLD

———————⊃⊙⊂———————

Tiahuanaco grew in size, splendour, and power as generation after generation passed. Its edifices were conceived
with a magnificent sweep of imagination. The materials of
which they were built were worked with exacting precision
and adorned with leisurely skill. The arts flourished and the
sciences throve. They found their consummate combined expression in the marvellous Calendar Gate of Kalasasaya. The
full significance of this most ancient human masterpiece of
chronography and sculpture will be discussed in Chapter 10.

The Asylum of Andinia was deemed to be safe from any
danger. But that dream of safety was suddenly interrupted. A
catastrophe occurred similar to that which generations before
undid the civilization of Huacullani and Simillake, and of the
Settlement near the Old Temple. The Inter-Andean Plateau
had again got 'below sea-level' through another unexpected
sudden and even more pronounced southward shift of the axis
of the girdle-tide. Again the waters surged into the Andinian
Asylum, leaping over parts of the mountain walls which were
of insufficient height, as well as racing in through the La Paz
gap, and perhaps also through the defiles near Ascotan, and
near Uyuni. But this time the waters came in greater quantity, and they came to stay. They engulfed an enormous area,
comprising Tiahuanaco and all the other culture-centres in the
Andinian Asylum, and formed a vast Sea—the Inter-Andean
Sea of the Highest Level. Not taking narrow fiord-like extensions into account, this sea was about 450 miles long and from
about 30 to 130 miles wide. It remained in communication with

the girdle-tide through the La Paz gap, and the Ascotan defile.
(Cf. the Map facing p. 14 and Diagram 11 facing p. 58.)

The suddenness of this flood catastrophe may be inferred
from the fact that no evidence of ancient strandlines is ascertainable between the littoral of the Inter-Andean Sea of the
Intermediate Level and the littoral of the new vast Inter-
Andean Sea of the Highest Level. Though unlike the conspicuously painted strandline of the Intermediate Level this
latter beach is not discernible from a distance, it is yet distinctly revealed to the closer investigator's eye by deposits of
great quantities of shells.

In the latitude of Tiahuanaco this highest strandline is 670
feet above the littoral of the Inter-Andean Sea of the Intermediate Level, or 760 feet above the present level of Lake
Titicaca, or 13,266 feet above sea-level. It is higher to the
north of Tiahuanaco and lower to the south, thus showing the
same peculiar slant as the strandline of the Intermediate
Level. This fact proves that the Inter-Andean Sea of the
Highest Level, too, was controlled by the gravitational pull of
the close Satellite.

There are evidences that immediately prior to this inundation there was a short period of tremendous volcanic activity.[29]
It was caused by the tension developing in the Earth's magma-
tic subcrust through the great precessional wobble, which,
when it had reached its maximum, had also brought about the
shift of the axis of the girdle-tide relative to the Andinian
Asylum. Tuffaceous layers of volcanic dust and ashes (*toba
volcanica*) are found in most parts of the region of the Tiahuanaco Asylum. In the immediate neighbourhood of the
volcanoes, banks up to 1,800, and even 2,000, feet thick are
occasionally to be observed, but towards the centre of the wide
Plateau the ash-layer (there later covered by alluvial deposits)
is much thinner, amounting generally to as little as about
two feet.

This ash-fall has preserved for us important proofs that once

69

a luxuriant, truly tropical vegetation existed in this region. For at many places a lignite-like layer of charred remains of plants has been found immediately underneath the greyish-white pall. On an average this layer of carbonized vegetation is four inches thick, but in many places it is considerably thicker, which proves the density of the former plant-life. Naturally it only occurs in areas which were situated above the surface of the Inter-Andean Sea of the Intermediate Level.

At many places the layer of volcanic ashes shows two different strata—a lower, softer one which was evidently originally deposited 'dry', and an upper, harder one which was evidently deposited 'wet'. The softer stratum represents the volcanic dust and ashes which fell and consolidated before the land above the strandline of the Inter-Andean Sea of the Intermediate Level was submerged; the harder stratum consists of the dust and ashes which fell into the waters of the Inter-Andean Sea of the Highest Level and eventually settled at the bottom.

The suddenness of the flood catastrophe which overwhelmed Tiahuanaco can be inferred from many evidences. Quantities of carefully worked stone blocks are lying about in different stages of completion. Tools were found near them, embedded in the soil, scattered as if they had been thrown down upon the impulse of an instant. Moulds are lying about for casting the bronze or copper cramps with which some of the megalithic masonry was bound. We find models of the principal buildings, or of parts of them, carefully worked in stone, lying tumbled about on that part of the site of Tiahuanaco which may have been the 'Office of Works'. Here and there considerable deposits are met with, containing bones of men and animals, fragments of pottery, beads, tools, etc., which have been washed away together.

The survivors of the great flood catastrophe which caused the end of Tiahuanaco and its sister centres apparently did not raise stone buildings any more, or their remains have not yet been discovered, for the region above the Highest Strand-line has hardly ever been investigated. Any ruins will have to be looked for rather far from the Highest Strandline, since the survivors probably did not trust the treacherous waters to build shore settlements and have harbour towns. Besides, it is to be supposed that most of the scientists and artists who lived in Tiahuanaco and in other settlements at or near the shore of the Inter-Andean Sea of the Intermediate Level perished when the waters rushed into the Asylum. The tillers of the andenes, on the other hand, who were much less advanced, remained safe, since they lived above the critical level.

The waters never rose beyond the strandline left by the Inter-Andean Sea of the Highest Level. The girdle-tide had by that time reached the greatest height which, for physical reasons, it was possible for it to reach, and the axis of the great tidal ring remained stable. At the bottom of the Inter-Andean Sea of the Highest Level lay, for a long time, the ruined, never finished edifices of Tiahuanaco. This prolonged submergence is proved by a shale-like layer of lime which is still adhering to some of the remains.

But there was another reason why the survivors of the flood catastrophe probably did not erect more substantial buildings than dugouts and log huts, and sought refuge chiefly in caves.[30] That reason was that 'soon' after the time of the great precessional wobble of the Earth which had caused the girdle-tide to flood the Inter-Andean Asylum, the Satellite entered the 'zone of the critical distance'. The disruptive powers of the terrestrial gravitation began to outweigh the cohesive powers of the Satellite, and it began to disintegrate. At first the satellitic material—ice, rock, and ore blocks—swung round the Earth in a sort of ring. This débris felt the resistance of the inter-planetary medium very strongly and approached the Earth rapidly on spiral paths. Hidden in the caves of the safe eastern side of the highest ridges of the Andes the refugees watched, fear-stricken, the breakdown of the Satellite, with its wind

71

storms, rain deluges, hail catastrophes, mud falls, core-block bombardment, earthquake throes, and volcanic paroxysms. This was the beginning of the great Age of Darkness, *Chamak-Pacha*, when the Sun was lost, of which the mythology of the Urus tells, and of which they say that it happened after the rise, and the loss, of Tiahuanaco. In spite of the violence of the cataclysm many of the refugees got through the apocalyptic upheaval unharmed, for the cosmic missiles, coming on practically tangential paths from the west, hardly ever hit their places of refuge, which were, so to speak, situated in the lee. Indeed, myths recorded in the Tiahuanaco region fully support these speculations. After a 'great flood' which happened in the times of old, we are told, the country was populated again by men and women who 'came out of caves, from the hills, from out of the waters, and from out of tree-trunks'. This latter statement must be taken to refer to wooden vessels of some description. That the Tiahuanacans had efficient ones we know from the fact of their transporting huge cargoes of bulky blocks of building material from a considerable distance.

For reasons which cannot be discussed here, most of the Satellite's wreckage fell on the African hemisphere of the Earth and much of it into the great girdle-tide. But quite a few blocks must have hit the Asylum, and some seem to have fallen into the Inter-Andean Sea. For some huge blocks of hitherto unidentified rock are found sticking in the practically absolute plain of 'alluvial soil' of the Inter-Andean Meseta. They have been described as 'blocks of conglomerate' and are believed to have been carried into the Meseta by glaciers, but they are quite un-Andean in type, and appear, moreover, to be partly vitrified on the outside. This latter fact is by some attributed to 'igneous' or 'volcanic' action, though the nearest volcanoes (now extinct) are scores of miles distant. We may, with much more likelihood, regard them as cosmic missiles, blocks of material from the topmost crust of the former Satellite's mineral body which had plunged into the waters of the girdle-tide, sunk to the bottom, and settled in the mud there.

72

After this cosmic uproar had been going on for some time an amazing thing happened: The Sea began to sink.

For, the Satellite's pull gone, the tropical water-belt of the girdle-tide ebbed off north and south in terrific ring-waves. Also the waters of the Inter-Andean Sea, whose peculiar level was not the result of geophysical reasons but the consequence of the Satellite's gravitational pull, became redistributed. They sank in the north and rose in the south of the Altiplano. In the north of the Meseta, Lake Titicaca soon came into existence with practically its present extent and general aspect. In the south of the Asylum, on the other hand, even more land was temporarily submerged through this redistribution of the waters, and a vast Poöpo-Coipasa-Uyuni-Sea was formed. The levels of this new Post-Diluvial Inter-Andean Sea, and Lake Titicaca, were 'straight', that is, they followed the geoidal curvature of the globe only. The two sheets of water were connected by the Desaguadero, which, for a considerable time, still carried much more water than it does now. (Cf. the Map facing page 14.)

With the end of the girdle-tide, the Andean Refuge 'rose' out of the waters and expanded into a wide continent. The same thing happened to all other tropical Asylums in the world.

But the joy of the survivors about the gaining of vast new life-space was only short-lived: for they suddenly felt with terror that the atmosphere became thin and icy.[31] The tropical warm 'air-tide', too, had flowed off, and their Asylum, in the latitude of Tiahuanaco, had 'risen' at least 16,000 feet[32] above sea-level. The only salvation now lay in speedy flight. In a world which writhed under the earthquakes caused by the breakdown cataclysm, and which was terribly lighted by the pillars of flame belching from the furiously active volcanoes, the survivors descended, gasping for air, numbed with cold, as quickly as possible to the lower outer slopes of the Andes. They followed the path whither the waters had gone. It led into a waste—but one which was soon to become another tropical paradise.

It was in this period of emigration that remnants of the formal elements of the Tiahuanaco culture reached the lower-lying territories towards the east, and the Pacific coast. Chiefly the style of pottery, that most easily transplanted domestic craft, found its way out of the Tiahuanaco Asylum, lingered on for a while, degenerated and finally died when new cultural impulses were created by the new natural and national surroundings, and all the manifold changes that these brought about.

The new Post-Diluvian Inter-Andean Sea which filled the southern part of the Inter-Andean Altiplano did not leave a strandline, because its level sank too quickly and progressively.

First of all, most of the water which had surged into the Inter-Andean Basin when breakers of the girdle-tide leaped over parts of the mountain-walls of the Asylum and cascades of water raced in through the defiles of La Paz, Ascotan, and Uyuni, poured out again through these gaps when the Satellite was no more.

Terrific deluge spates cascaded down into the lower-lying lands in the east and west which had just emerged out of the receding waters of the ebbing girdle-tide. The surplus waters of the Inter-Andean Sea of the Highest Level surged between the mountain-range which culminates in the Illimani and the Cordillera de Aráca down the narrow gorges of La Paz, into the Upper Amazon (Beni and Madeira) region, and eventually out into the newly formed 'Atlantic Ocean'. East of Uyuni, between the Cordillera de Chicas and the Cordillera de Choc-aya, the waters poured down into the Upper Parana (Pilcomayo, Bermejo, and Paraguay) region, and thus also finally into the 'Atlantic'. And in the south-west of the Inter-Andean Basin the waters raced through the narrow defile of Ascotan, which was more than a hundred miles long, almost directly down into the newly formed 'Pacific'. (Cf. the Map facing page 14 and Diagram 11 facing p. 58.)

THE END OF A WORLD

These deluge spates, cascading down from the heights of the
Andes for many weeks, must have been terrific. Let us for a
moment consider the work done by that which raced through
the La Paz gap and washed out what are now the towering cliffs
of the gorges of the Rio de La Paz, which cleave the imposing
mountain-mass of the Cordillera Real. From stratigraphic
evidence it appears that about 6000 feet of strata have been cut
through—a task which cannot possibly be placed to the credit of
the rather insignificant Rio de La Paz. To erode these gorges
incredible volumes of water carrying immense quantities of
loose abrasive material must have shot out from the Altiplano
towards the south-east. The country looks as if an army of
Titans had thrown everything into the weirdest confusion.
Everywhere there are vast cones of talus; they are rich in ores
and huge blocks of rock are stuck in the rubble and loam. On
the granite spurs of the mighty Illimani, which towers to more
than 21,000 feet, at the mouth of the valley of La Paz, the
turbid tide seems to have broken its chief force; it was also
turned towards the north-east, and finally ebbed off, more
leisurely, into the plains of the Beni and Madeira branches of
the Amazon. 'Thus', says Neveu-Lemaire in his book about
the hydrography of the Altiplano, 'the greatest inland sea of
the Earth fed with its waters the greatest river in the world'
for a time in the past.

Geologists frequently ascribe the state of things in the La Paz
region to the action of glaciers. But the aspect of the country
shows that it must have been a fluviatile catastrophe which did
quick work on a tremendous scale, rather than slow glacial
action extending over long spells of time. A fluviatile catastrophe, however, presupposes conditions such as we have outlined in the preceding paragraphs.

The level of what remained of the Post-Cataclysmic Inter-
Andean Sea after all the surplus waters had flowed off through
the different defiles fell rather quickly. The Inter-Andean
Basin being self-contained, it depended entirely upon the

precipitation in its catchment area to offset the losses through evaporation. As this precipitation was probably never greater than it is now, the level of the remains of the great Sea became steadily lower.

No strandlines tell of this stage. They can only come into being when there is sufficient time available, and the fall of the water-level then was both progressive and rapid.

As we have just seen, a smaller Northern Basin (practically the present Lake Titicaca) and a very much bigger Southern Basin (covering the whole Poöpo-Coipasa-Uyuni area) developed after the end of the Inter-Andean Sea of the Highest Level. As nearly all the rivers (as now) flowed into the Titicaca Basin, it remained in permanent connexion with the Poöpo-Coipasa-Uyuni Basin through what is now called the Desaguadero River. The feeders of Lake Titicaca naturally being fresh, it became less and less salty in the course of time. Drainage through the Uyuni and Ascotan gaps as long as the level of the water was high enough, and eventually the great and progressive desiccation, caused the salty Southern Basin soon to split into a Poöpo-Coipasa Part and an Uyuni Part. Finally all the Uyuni Part, and most of the Poöpo-Coipasa Part, dried up, and vast salt-deserts came into being—the Salar of Coipasa, and the Salar of Uyuni with its appendages, the small Salares of Empexa, Coposa, Chiguana, Ollagüe, Carcote, and Ascotan. In these salt-deserts were still set the last shallow remains of the former Sea, the present Lakes Poöpo and Coipasa. Thus finally the state was reached which the physiography of the Inter-Andean Basin still shows at the present day.

With the 'rise' of the Tiahuanaco Asylum its climate changed radically. Whatever animals and plants could not stand the rapid change in temperature, oxygenation, radiation, etc., died at once, while those which could began to degenerate in their unpropitious environment. They became stunted and developed primitive aspects. Judging from fossils

76

the Titicaca fishes were formerly about five times as big as they are now. The same refers to other animals, and also to plants.

It is no idle romance to ascribe the end of Tiahuanaco and the other culture centres on the shore of the Inter-Andean Sea of the Intermediate Level to a great inundation catastrophe caused by a southward shift of the axis of the girdle-tide. We are quite positive when we say that the confusion which the archaeologist's spade discovers there is not man-caused. It was not political agitation which made the workers down their tools, and abandon their unfinished tasks forever. It was not popular discontent and civil war which caused the hand that had held the chisel to grasp more sinister weapons. It was not a revolution of oppressed slaves which was doomed to eventual utter failure after all the educated had perished in a welter of blood. It was not a jealous enemy descending from the uplands with trumpets blaring and banners flying to wipe out the great new city of man which was just building. We can confidently say that it *was* a cosmic cause. We can also confidently say that it *was* the former Satellite. For on the pottery found in the soil of Tiahuanaco are frequently to be seen significant representations of a certain heavenly body which, as it is depicted as a yellow—that is, glaringly bright—disk, has been interpreted as the Sun. It cannot stand for the Sun,[33] however, because the Tiahuanacans would certainly not have painted that beneficent power in connexion with the determinative pictograph of the fierce, treacherous Puma, the symbol and personification of fear, evil, and danger.

No—the Puma-Star can only be the former Satellite which had caused so much havoc already and which, it was feared, might prove even more dangerous still. This interpretation alone fits into the mosaic of manifold facts which have been established regarding Tiahuanaco and its realm.

And it was indeed the Puma-Star which eventually caused the end of Tiahuanaco.

THE END OF A WORLD

The redistribution of the waters in the Altiplano made emerge again the submerged ruins of Tiahuanaco, which had been 670 feet below the surface of the Inter-Andean Sea of the Highest Level. The halls and the mazes of megalithic masonry, which for a long time had housed, if anything at all, only a scanty deep-sea life, were now invaded by shyly scurrying or leisurely roaming land animals. For immense reaches of time yet, however, no man's footstep woke the silent echoes which slumbered in the dead walls.

Tiahuanaco was completely forgotten. The few descendants of the survivors of the great cataclysm who had stayed in the highlands and eked out a meagre and depressed existence there shunned the site regarding which their traditions told a terrible tale of dangers and destruction. And those distant descendants of the survivors who had left the Asylum and now lived, great and populous nations, in the luxuriant tropical lowlands and among the fertile temperate foothills of the Andes, had probably forgotten all about the actual existence of Tiahuanaco and regarded it as little more than a 'myth'. They probably never attempted the ascent of the mighty, snow-topped, ice-embattled, mountain wall, whose highest peaks at that time[32] towered to some 27,000 feet above the sea-level of the latitude of about ten degrees south. There was absolutely no need for such a mountaineering feat. The thin air, the cruel cold, the complete barrenness of the uplands, on the one hand, did not attract curious rovers, and, on the other, definitely opposed any inquisitive, straying people, hunters, and the like.

Yet, as time passed, such need began to arise. For, at certain times, when a particular outer planet shone especially bright in the heavens, the waters of the Pacific (and all the other oceans of the Earth) swelled, and great tidal waves washed far beyond the wonted shores. Such encroachments occurred again and again, and with greater and greater vehemence, at every conjunction of the Earth with the small outer planet. At last the authorities of the prehistoric realms which then flourished in the regions affected by the tides grasped the real meaning of these phenomena, discovered their cause, and became aware of the terrible danger which was threatening. Then it was found that the traditions, sagas, and myths of the great time of stress in the past—which had become little more than indistinctly murmured nursery tales, and mechanically babbled liturgical texts, during the quiet paradisial period after the breakdown of the former Satellite—contained important truths. The ancient reports told that in the past salvation from the waters had been found in the heights, whence their forefathers had descended, and where now their gods dwelt, keeping ready a splendid home for those who would avail themselves of it.

So scouts were sent out, and behind the icy barriers they discovered the world-lost site of Tiahuanaco with its great remains. The temples and other edifices were standing a few miles from the then shore of Lake Titicaca, and the region, though bleak, seemed capable of development. It had grown somewhat warmer there, for the air-blanket of the Earth had become enriched again after the great impoverishment which had taken place during the cataclysm caused by the former Satellite. The re-discoverers of Tiahuanaco must have gained the impression that the site was absolutely safe for settlement, and that the culture of the threatened lower regions might be transferred there. This happened something like 13,500 years ago.

But these plans were never carried out. For the cosmic event happened from whose direct consequences the people of the Asatellitic Age had wanted to escape.

The scientists of the latter stages of the Moonless Aeon had foreseen the eventual capture of the planet Luna and the terrific tidal catastrophe it would entail. But they had probably not calculated that the capture cataclysm would happen as soon as it did.

When Luna was deprived of its independence as a planet it

probably shot by very close to the Earth. At its first perigee, certainly the closest of all, the distance of the new Satellite from our Earth was perhaps only one half of the present mean distance of our Moon, which is 60 Earth radii. The most terrific gravitational pull which it was thus able to wield threw all the waters of the Earth suddenly into the tropics. A series of annular eagres, globe-girdling tidal ring-waves, mountain-high, steeply reared, rushed in roaring career towards the equator. There the waters from the northern and southern hemispheres met and rose to a great height. When the impetus of the first onrush was spent, most of the waters swung back again, ebbing towards the poles. Moreover, the new Satellite was then already speeding away from the Earth, towards its first, and most distant, apogee, which may have reached, perhaps even exceeded, 80 Earth radii.

This great and sudden tide washed over islands and over the coastal regions of the continents. Whoever was in the danger areas was killed; whatever was there was destroyed. Probably most of those who were just actively planning to emigrate to the Inter-Andean Tableland found their death then.

Whether Tiahuanaco, or any part of the Inter-Andean Region, was ever settled by survivors of the great capture cataclysm when things had quietened down, we cannot tell. If so, they were probably too few to make real use of the remains in the Inter-Andean Basin, and to attempt to re-establish the culture of their lost homeland in the barren Tableland.

Such survivors or refugees soon lapsed into primitivism, and their descendants, perhaps intermingling with any sparse older settlers there, became the small tribes of tough, stolid Indians who still live in the Andean highlands, clinging to the wastes with a strange tenacity. These refugees evidently avoided—as the Indians still avoid—the lonely ruins, 'where the guanaco rested' in undisturbed peace.

The Incas who appeared in the Andean highlands from no one knows exactly where, but most probably from a lost land—

in ships, as their myths tell[34]—apparently took no, or only very little, interest in the ruins of Tiahuanaco and the other sites. They preferred to settle in a more northerly region, Cuzco, which was less elevated, easier of access, and much more fertile. They used the substructures of the megalithic buildings they found there, and based their own, different, masonry on them. When eventually small groups of Incas did come to live in the Titicaca Region they built their temples and other edifices well away from Tiahuanaco.

Apparently only the Spaniards decided to make an attempt to colonize the Meseta. Unluckily they used the ruins of Tiahuanaco as a builder's yard containing a wealth of squared stone, and carried off all that could conveniently be carried, thus destroying most of what the tooth of time had spared. That type of vandalism, unfortunately, is still in practice in our days.

In the foregoing we have traversed the vast arch of time which leads from the remote prehistoric period whose date is in the dim past, when Tiahuanaco was being built with so much art and skill, to our own days, when the pilfered site of the great metropolis shows little more than a few scattered stones. We have tried to answer a number of puzzling questions, though in doing so we have probably raised a host of others. Yet we believe we have opened new vistas for the archaeologist and the prehistorian, and blazed a path into the past which may be well worth considering and following up.

We do not know the real name of the ancient city on the shore of the Inter-Andean Sea of the Intermediate Strandline, which we called Tiahuanaco. Its echo does not resound any more in the megalithic ruins. Also of the builders we know nothing. Their race, their tongue, who can determine them? Do Quechua and Aymara treasure echoes of the accents of the lost speech of the Andinian Asylum?[35] Are the Indians who speak these languages the direct descendants of survivors from the cataclysms which overwhelmed the different cultures that flourished in the Inter-Andean Asylum? We can tell from a number of the portrait heads which have been found that some of the Tiahuanacans, the nobles perhaps, practised the enlargement of the lobes of the ears, as the later rulers of Peru did, or as the megalithic *moai* statues of mysterious Easter Island show. Also the artificial elongation of the skull was practised. But these and similar evidences are too slender and general to build a racial theory on. Nor would any such theory be of much real value; for it is evident that the region of Tiahuanaco has been a gathering-place for a variety of races. Indeed, the Andean Altiplano appears to have been, even if not one of the cradles of Man, then certainly one of his great refuges in times of cosmic stress, and one of the nurseries of the arts and sciences. The human remains[36] which have been found in the main culture strata together with the bones of the toxodon, which is said to have died out in Tertiary Times, do not seem to belong to a homogeneous people. That is why we said that congregations of nations must have met there, that is why we talked of convocations of workers, architects, scientists, artists, gathering together from all over the lessening living space of that part of the Earth. Their achievements presuppose an extremely high technical development, and the elaboration of efficient tools and tackle. The style of their architecture is powerful, 'modern', because of the sparing use of figurative ornamentation, and the pronounced endeavour to let the material 'speak for itself'. This architecture has been specially evolved to suit the conditions which then obtained in the world. The art and science of the Tiahuanacans, chiefly as revealed by the Great Gate of the Sun Temple of Kalasasaya, with its marvellous sculptured 'Calendar', were profound. This forces us to the conclusion that the leading class, at least, must have been of gentle race—a flower of humanity. They were more than builders, they were impatient rebuilders of the culture of a lost home. This is no idle fancy of ours. For in the clayey soil of Tiahuanaco were found what seem to be the portrait heads of the great men of that time. They show high foreheads, open faces, bold profiles, energetic chins. There is especially one head—that of a dignitary, probably, because of his cap of office—which is unforgettable. It is unfinished, but this makes it all the more impressive. For it seems to force its proud face powerfully out of the rude, hard stone, as if impatient with the sculptor's slow chisel, as if knowing that only thus its likeness should not vanish, but endure for the ages.

10

THE CALENDAR OF KALASASAYA

The assertion that the slanting strandline upon which the
enigmatic ruins of Tiahuanaco are situated was formed
at a time when another satellite dominated the heavens sounds
so extravagant that the reasoning mind refuses to accept it.
For if this assertion is allowed, the prehistoric Andinian
Metropolis must be hundreds of thousands of years old,
certainly not less than a quarter of a million! For the archaeologist who avoids exceeding about 5000 B.C. in his dating of
early human achievements, for the anthropologist who con-
ceives Man to have been a shambling brute a hundred thousand years ago, and for the geologist who fears that we want to
carry catastrophistic revolution into his quietistic realm, our
idea must be staggering.

In defending ourselves against the accusation that we are
mere idle romancers, if not worse, we must seek to support our
argument not with any trend of reasoning taken from Hoerbiger's Theory of Satellites—although, of course, we may
legitimately retain this as our ultimate working hypothetical
basis. We must support it instead with something which is
taken from the culture-circle of the lost city itself. We must
seek our witness, so to speak, among the Tiahuanacans.

By chance so rare as almost to make us wonder if it be
chance, or if it be the design of a Higher Entity, we can cite an
unimpeachable witness of insistent speech—a 'Calendar'.

Upon the ruin-field of Tiahuanaco, half buried in hardened
grey mud, riven but resolute by dint of its mass, there was
found the great Gateway which obviously led originally to a

84

very important part of the Sun Temple of Kalasasaya.[37] This pylon is not only a triumph of megalithic architecture, being hewn out of *one block* of almost glass-hard andesite, about 10 feet high, 12½ feet wide, 1½ feet thick, and weighing about ten tons;[38] it is also a marvel of sculpture, for the upper part of the front of this massive portal is encrusted with stupendously rich and beautifully executed carvings, while its back is adorned with well-balanced niches and escalinated cornices.[39] (Cf. Diagrams 12 and 13 on p. 87.)

General Analysis of the Calendar Sculpture

At first sight the beholder of this impressive relief might be led to judge, from its wealth of imagery and the symmetric arrangement and general lay-out of its constituents, that it is merely ornamental. On closer acquaintance, however, it is soon realized that the glyphs must have an ideographic meaning. Because of their arrangement they cannot constitute a 'historical inscription'. Indeed, soon after their discovery the idea was put forward that the glyphs constituted a 'Calendar'—but all attempts to decipher it, all endeavours to make it speak, have hitherto been in vain. Not even the most eminent and resourceful specialists in chronography were able to coax the secrets of its peculiar method of notation out of the plastic symbolism of the reticent stone calendar of Tiahuanaco.

All that the analysis of the calendar sculpture yielded is: that the Calendar of Tiahuanaco is a mere 'counting calendar'; that, hence, it does not reveal the 'time basis' upon which, or the 'zero year' in which, it was established; that it does not record any definite 'date' whatsoever; and that its symbolism apparently cannot be used for the expression of dates. From the form of the Calendar follows that the year of the Tiahuanacans shows twelve subdivisions, or 'months', if we employ the nomenclature of our own time-charts; that the beginning of the year is distinctly designated; that the equinoxes are unmistakably shown; and that the solstices are most characteristically marked. From these latter points it follows, finally, that the year of the Tiahuanacans shown on the Calendar of Kalasasaya was a Solar Year.

This, in fact, is much more than the Calendars of our own time show at a glance. But when the attempt was made to reconcile the number of days in the 'Tiahuanaco year' and the 'Tiahuanaco months' with the number of days in our own, or

---

DIAGRAM 12

Elevation of the front of the monolithic Calendar Gate
of the Temple of Kalasasaya in Tiahuanaco.

To stress the classic form of the gate the reliefs have here been eliminated. The First Twelfth and its pedestal fill the upright rectangular space in the centre, the meander frieze with the eleven other twelfths takes up the long rectangular space immediately above the door opening (cf. Diagram 23). The three times five practically square small spaces above this band, and to the right and left of the space occupied by the First Twelfth contain the winged figures shown in Diagram 20. The remaining rectangular and square spaces contain more winged figures and mirrored repetitions of the meander frieze, the part squares proving that the sculpture was continued on the right and left. How far it was thus continued is not ascertainable. (It will be appreciated that the artistic impression would be better without these repetitive continuations.)[39a]

DIAGRAM 13

Elevation of the back of the monolithic gate.

The two big shallow niches must have been closed by massive 'doors', or shutters, of some sort, as is proved by the damage caused by the wrenching out of the pins or pivots on which they swung. The damage at the base of the gate was caused by the monolith being wrenched off the pins or cramps with which it was fastened to its foundation.[39b]

Scale in feet.

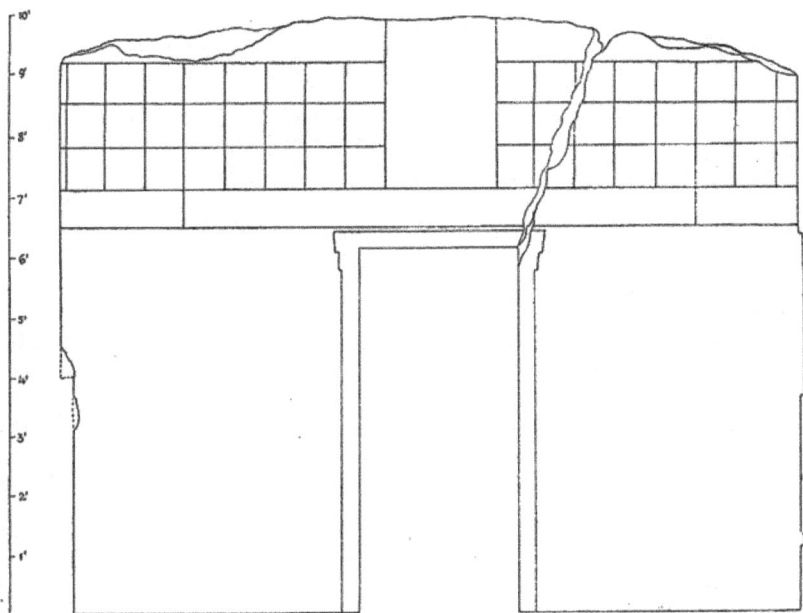

DIAGRAM 12

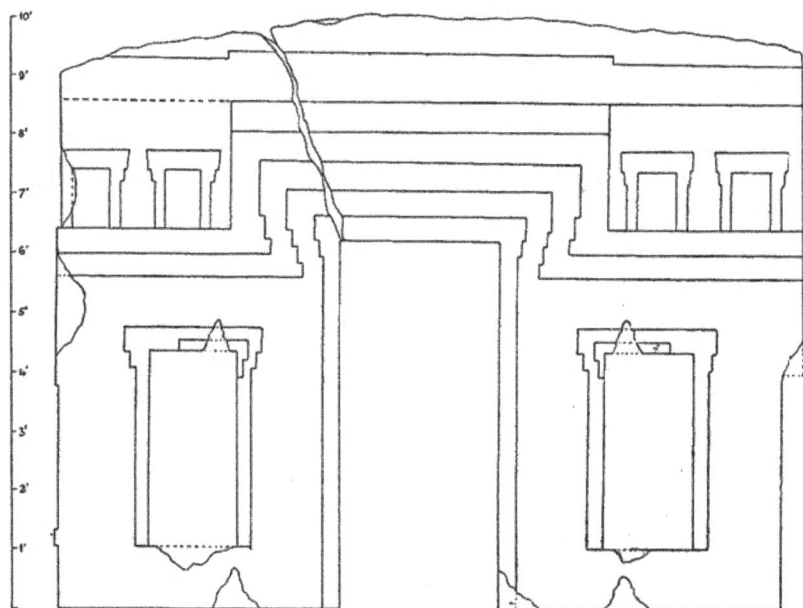

DIAGRAM 13

any other known or conceivable year and months, insurmountable difficulties arose.

All investigators have hitherto got hopelessly stuck at this point.

Before we proceed let us consider some of the problems of calendar making.

What points must a calendar maker observe if he wishes to construct a time-chart? How should an efficient time-chart look?

The most essential points to be observed when devising a calendar are:

1. It must be easily legible, 'at a glance', by people with only an average education (farmers, craftsmen, etc.);
2. It must be correct—though necessarily, of course, only for the time when it was established;
3. It must reveal, to the knowing eye at least, the time when it was in use;
4. It must show the cosmic body or bodies on the observation of whose movements it was based, or it should, at least, readily allow such identification.

Point 1 is self-evident, for we cannot imagine that the makers of any calendar would compile a picture-puzzle of rebuses which could only be interpreted by the specially initiated few—the priests, scientists, etc. However enigmatic and involved the design may appear to us it must have been easily 'read' by the people for whom it was devised—the common people, who formed the majority of those who frequented the Temple of Kalasasaya. This does not, of course, exclude the possibility that the sculpture also contained 'esoteric' material.

Point 2 is also self-evident. Calendars are made to determine certain supremely important times of the year. The provisioning of as numerous a population as that of the realm of Tiahuanaco required a highly organised feeding

industry. Sowing and reaping, stockbreeding, fishing, hunting, are all tied to definite seasons, not to say special dates,
even in 'tropical' regions: hence the need for an efficient
calendar. The clause allows for any changes which may have
occurred in the time-reckoning basis since the calendar was
established.

From Point 3 it follows that the Calendar of Tiahuanaco
must not be compared with our own calendar, nor with any
other calendar, which is or was in use anywhere else in the
world. It must be allowed to speak for itself, though this, of
course, should stand to reason without our stressing it. All
that can be, and has already been, established by comparison
with other time-reckoning systems is that the Calendar of
Kalasasaya can *not* be reconciled with any hitherto known
year, nor with any which, up till now, could be conceived in
theory.

Point 4 is also obvious, for the calendar of a people of culture
and civilization cannot be the result of a whim of a political or
religious dictator, but must be based on regularly recurring
cosmic events, the actual or apparent motion both of the Earth
and of extra-terrestrial bodies, i.e. events which allow time-
calculation and time-checking. From point 2 would follow that
also the Tiahuanaco year must have been ultimately based on
the revolution of the Earth round the Sun.

Our own (Christian, Jewish, Mohammedan, etc.) calendars
show the number of days in the year, which, of course, is the
most important thing for a calendar to do. All other features
are purely conventional and merely introduced for the sake of
convenience—though it is highly problematic whether they
are always convenient. Thus our calendars show 'months',
which, however, contrary to the derivation and meaning of the
word, have not now, and probably never had, anything to do
with the Moon as to their length and beginning.[40] The 'weeks'
of our calendars were originally, as is still shown by the etymo-
logical meaning of their name, the 'change times' of the two

89

chief phases of the Moon,[41] but have long lost this connexion, and also, therefore, any real sense and significance.

While our calendars show these unimportant conventional sub-divisions of the year, they do not show any of the logically important ones, such as the four seasons and their beginning. It might, of course, be argued that 'everybody knows that anyhow'. Furthermore, the year of our calendars, while actually a solar year, 'begins' on an indifferent day, instead of at the Spring Equinox, or, alternatively, the Winter Solstice.

The most important thing, therefore, which our own calendar clearly shows, is the number of days. Hence, assuming that the calendar-makers of Tiahuanaco also attributed the main importance to the number of days in the year we must turn our attention chiefly to this point.

The followers of Hoerbiger's Cosmological Theory say that the Tiahuanaco of the Calendar Gate flourished at the time towards the end of the Aeon of the predecessor of our present Moon. This fact can hardly be assailed. For only when we claim that the Andinian Metropolis and port existed at the time of the girdle-tide can we link it with the slanting strand-line. And much more important: only when we attribute so remote a 'date' to the Calendar of Kalasasaya does it begin not only to speak, but to speak readily, clearly, and intelligibly.

An investigator is entitled to use any trend of reasoning which he believes will lead him to a solution of his problem. If his theory and the facts before him do not—completely, or at least very largely—coincide, the theory must be dropped; if they do, the theory, however strange and unorthodox it may be, must be allowed to be the true explanation of the facts.

Before we proceed we shall have to put the following questions, which are of absolute importance.[42]

1. Is the 'Solar Year' an absolute unit of time, which has always had, and will always have, the same length (expressed in *hours of present length*[43]) as now? If not, was it longer or shorter in the distant past?

90

THE CALENDAR OF KALASASAYA

2. Was the Solar Year of that time, whatever its length, divided into $365\frac{1}{4}$ days like that of our time, or had it a smaller number of longer, or a greater number of shorter, days?

3. The 'Year' of the Calendar of Kalasasaya is divided into twelve parts. Is each of these twelve parts a genuine month (i.e. having the length, or approximate length, of one real, or apparent, revolution of the Satellite round the Earth) or are they arbitrary divisions with no such significance, like our own 'months'?

4. If the 'Twelfths' do not signify real, or apparent, revolutions of the Satellite round the Earth, does the Stone Calendar show the actual number of these?

Let us defer the answers to these questions till a little later.

When Edmund Kiss, a German cosmologist of note, visited the site of Tiahuanaco in the years 1928 and 1929 for a personal detailed survey of its ruins and the intensive study of their problems, Professor Arthur Posnansky, who has been interested in the (hitherto only very desultory) excavations in the Tiahuanaco area for more than forty years, told him in despair, that he had devoted a life-time to the unriddling of the secrets of that region, but that he had not been able to come even within sight of a solution, notwithstanding all his endeavours. The Stone Calendar on the Gate of the Sun Temple of Kalasasaya had been the greatest and most intriguing of all these puzzles.

The despondency of Professor Posnansky is deplorable, for he marches far ahead of all other Americanists and prehistorians, and is not timid regarding the explanation of the observed facts. One cannot help feeling sorry for him, for the satisfactory unravelling of the mysteries of the Andinian Metropolis would give him new powers. His own ill success hitherto is only due to the thought-tool, or theory, which he employs, and which is—to say the least offensive thing about it—out of date. One cannot unlock the portals of the past with the picklocks of the present! Every door has its own particular key.

91

Edmund Kiss went to Tiahuanaco well supplied with efficient tools of the correct type. Steeped in the thought-world of Hoerbiger's Cosmological Theory, and, moreover, armed with certain of Hoerbiger's unique calculations (cf. pp. 104 foll.), he was able to attack the problem so successfully from a new angle that by 1934 he was in a position to declare most of the puzzles of Tiahuanaco practically solved. The interpretation of the Calendar sculpture on the gateway of Kalasasaya was the most important result of his endeavours. In 1937, after the mature reconsideration of all his investigations, calculations, and deductions, he published his findings in the excitingly interesting, well illustrated work already mentioned above: *Das Sonnentor von Tihuanaku*.

Kiss's solution of the fundamental problems of the Tiahuanaco Calendar is one of the masterpieces of the application of Hoerbiger's Theory of Satellites. It is even more. It has in its turn proved to be an important support for the Theory itself. But of this the reader must judge for himself.

It was to be expected that Kiss's findings would eventually have to be modified when new investigators undertook a new analysis of the Calendar of Kalasasaya. However, it was found that Kiss's errors mostly relate to minor details only: his basis is sound and will always remain so. And it was his sound findings which made possible the further analysis and interpretation of the calendar sculpture which is offered in this book.

The sculptured upper part of the monolithic gateway of the Sun Temple of Kalasasaya appears very complicated and involved at first sight—but after even a very short analysis it resolves itself into perfectly clear separate constituents.[44]

The first fact which becomes evident is that the relief consists of an essential central part and of unimportant lateral extensions. The latter are only repetitions of the important central part, and while that is beautifully carved the lateral extensions are only roughly traced out and in every sense 'unfinished'.[45] (On Diagram 23, at the end of the book, these repetitive extensions have been eliminated, but Diagram 12, on p. 87, will give an idea as to their extent.)

On scanning the beautifully and delicately executed central part of the sculpture it is soon appreciated that it consists of two different matters which though they must eventually be related are obviously not immediately and intimately so.

A strikingly commanding figure, apparelled in rich cere-monial robes and holding insignia of power or of rank in its hands,[46] is depicted standing on a high pedestal of peculiar form. This pedestal rests on a marvellously conceived meander whose bays contain eleven curious heads, or faces. This consti-tutes the one matter. (Diagram 23.)

The other matter consists of two 'panels' of fifteen closely grouped winged figures each (cf. Diagram 20, on p. 129) which are placed above the meander-line on either side of the central figure and its pedestal.

When we now turn our full attention to the great meander-line and the central figure on its pedestal which dominates it— we gain almost immediately the impression that it must be this part of the sculpture which refers to the year of the Tiahuanacans. This impression, though it may at first have been due to subjective reasoning, is soon confirmed by objec-tive facts. For on further analysis we notice a number of quite unequivocal 'Reading Helps', or 'Pointers', which the origin-ator of this marvellous sculpture incorporated into his design to help anyone who beholds it—his contemporaries in the first instance, and us in the last—to 'read' the symbolism of the calendar easily and correctly.

From the outward form of the Calendar (cf. Diagram 23) follows with absolute certainty that the Tiahuanacans divided their year into twelve parts as we do ours. Yet the similarity is only superficial: as will soon be shown, the subdivisions of the two calendar systems have nothing in common except the denominator. We shall therefore call these subdivisions 'Twelfths' in this disquisition, to differentiate them sharply from the twelve 'Months' into which we divide our own year.

The central figure tells us by its size, position, and special execution that it represents the first and most important Twelfth. It designates evidently a Twelfth commencing with an equinox, admittedly a rational or logical beginning of the Year.

This supposition was at first only put forward tentatively: but with the aid of various 'reading helps' it was soon substantiated. The First Twelfth of the Tiahuanaco Calendar *must* start with an equinoctial point because of its balanced position. The question which point of Day-and-Night-Balance it was cannot apparently be decided from the symbolism of the Calendar. However, on thorough analysis of all the calendar problems it transpired beyond doubt that it was the *autumnal* one. (Cf. pp. 149 foll. and Note 67.)

The first day of the First Twelfth of the Calendar of Kalasasaya—New Year's Day, so to speak—was the Day of the Autumn Equinox, comparable to our March 21st. With us in the northern hemisphere spring begins on this day, but in the southern half of the globe, where Tiahuanaco is situated, it marks the beginning of autumn.[47] The First Twelfth of the Tiahuanaco Year ran, using our own calendar and our present date of the equinox in question, from March 21st to April 20th.

If our interpretation of the central figure as that of the 'Twelfth of the Autumn Equinox' is correct, then the 'head' in the same balanced central position immediately under it must represent the 'Twelfth of the Spring Equinox' (September 23rd to October 22nd of our own calendar). (Cf. Diagram 14 on p. 97.)[48] The fact that the head of the Seventh Twelfth is placed upon a pedestal of *three* steps, like the figure of the First Twelfth, definitely 'points' to such a connexion. The First and the Seventh Twelfths are also connected by the fact that both feature the non-numerical symbol No. 2, the former on its body, the latter on its pedestal. Besides its importance is also stressed by the seventh head being of greater size than that of the ten other Twelfths. Like the head of the First Twelfth it has none of the additional crownlike ornaments or determinators which the other ten heads show. The first and seventh

94

heads were evidently intended to 'speak for themselves'. They are distinguished by nothing but their position.

The meander which nooses in the eleven 'heads' in the bottom line of the Calendar relief is delimited on either side by energetically upraised, crested and crowned heads of the sacred *Kunturi Mayku*.[49] These personifications of the Sun, employed as authoritative 'pointers', inform us, firstly, that the actual Calendar, expressive of the solar year, is at an end here;[50] and, secondly, they point out to us that something relating to the Sun is to be found at these places. Logically we should expect the Solstices, the 'turning-points of the Sun', to be located here. Indeed, we are again helped by further unmistakable authoritative 'pointers', or reading helps, which confirm to us that our surmise is right. On either of the heads at the extreme left and right of the long bottom line of the Calendar we see a most grotesque little trumpeter, the one on the left ('Twelfth of the Winter Solstice', June 21st to July 20th in our reckoning) turning resolutely, and blowing vigorously, towards the right, and putting his significantly enlarged 'best foot' energetically forward in the same direction, while his equally quaint colleague on the right side ('Twelfth of the Summer Solstice', December 22nd to January 20th) does the exact opposite.[51] The one hand of either bugler holds his *khuepa* (Aymara for trumpet), the other grasps a human head—probably the head of the demon who tampers with the Sun and causes its unequal course in the year.

The solar significance of the two trumpeters is strongly stressed by significant determinative ornaments: they wear a toxodon's head in front of their elaborate 'caps'; a toxodon's head adorns the 'shoes' of their forward-stepping feet; and a condor's head hangs as a maniple from their elbows.[52] These symbols have been found to be solar ones. (Cf. Diagrams 15 and 16 on pp. 98 and 99.)

Thus the chief points of the Calendar are in their logical positions, indeed in the only ones really possible for them: The equinoxes, at which day and night are 'balanced', are in the centre, like the tongue and pivot of a balance, while the solstices are at either end of the beam.

Because of this arrangement of its major parts the Tiahuanaco Calendar *must* be expressive of the *solar* year, that is, of the natural year, not of any man-made shorter period. The symbolism is quite unmistakable and allows of no other interpretation.

Such an arrangement, however, does not allow the marshalling of the twelfth-heads in one line. The creator of the Calendar of Tiahuanaco, therefore, has devised an extremely simple and yet most ingenious and artistic scheme which permits both the arrangement of the eleven heads in one line and the balanced form above referred to. By means of a masterfully managed meander, he compels the reader of the Calendar to proceed, 'step by step', and to 'read' only those heads, one after the other, which are in the bays open on the side where the previous twelfth has been read. (Cf. the numbering in Diagram 23.) Four plain condor heads in each recess especially 'point' to each respective head.

The Calendar sculpture on the Sun Gate of Tiahuanaco is vigorous and living, in spite of its rigid symmetry and strict balance. It is chiefly the peculiarly spirited and senseful arrangement of the various elements which creates and stresses that impression.

From the fact that the Tiahuanaco Calendar is balanced upon the equinoctial points can be inferred—and the inference shows itself to be well substantiated on closer investigation—that the year at that time was symmetrical about the equinoxes, and asymmetrical about the solstices. In the year of our time practically the exact reverse is the case. The only possible explanation of this peculiarity is that, when the calendar was designed, the Earth's apses coincided with the equinoxes, instead of being close to the solstices as they are now.

So far the analysis of the Tiahuanaco Calendar into its greater constituents, seasons and twelfths, has been natural and simple. We have found that the stone time-chart, in spite

DIAGRAM 14. THE SEVENTH TWELFTH
or Twelfth of the Vernal Equinox ('September–October').
Actual size.

97

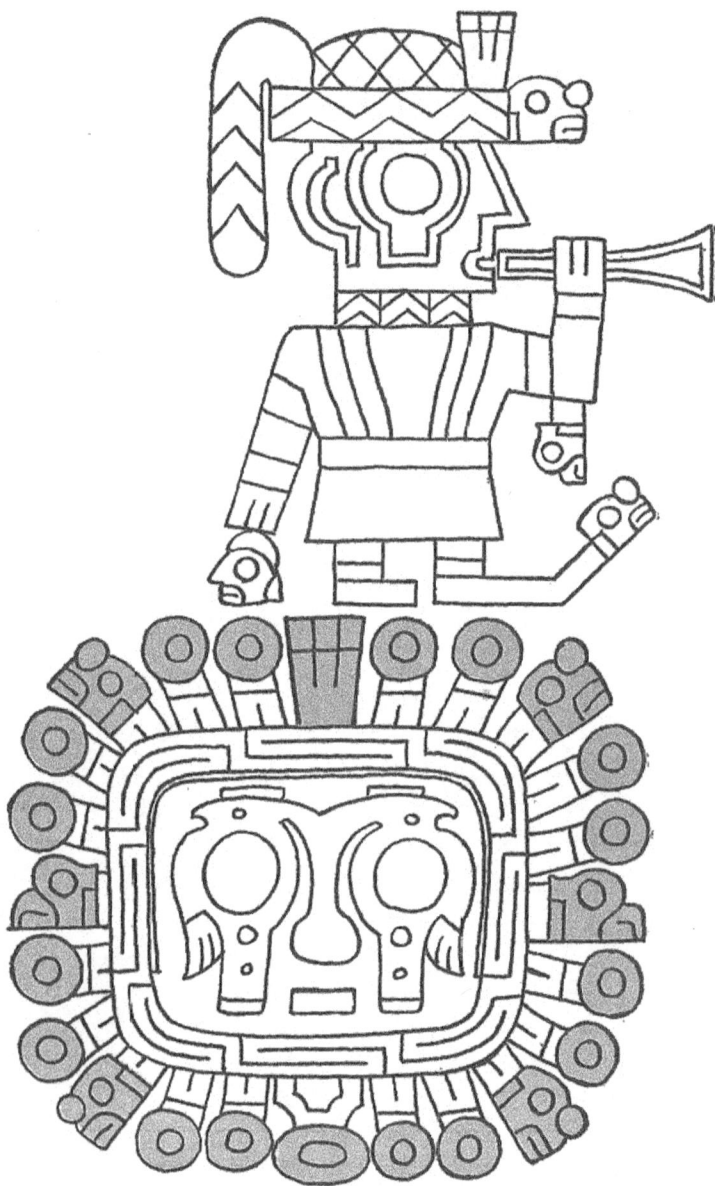

DIAGRAM 15. THE FOURTH TWELFTH
or Twelfth of the Winter Solstice ('June–July').
Actual size.

98

DIAGRAM 16. THE TENTH TWELFTH
or Twelfth of the Summer Solstice ('December–January').
Actual size.

of its—at first sight—most unfamiliar and apparently extremely complicated form, has revealed itself as being quite easily intelligible. We have also found that it is exceedingly cleverly devised, and that it contains incomparably more detail that can be gathered at a glance than our own rather awkward and ugly day and month tables.

When comparing the First Twelfth with the Seventh Twelfth, and with the remaining ten Twelfths, it is immediately seen that obviously only the 'haloes' of symbols round the 'faces' must be taken into consideration with reference to the solar year, while all the 'extras', on the body and the pedestal of the First Twelfth, and on the heads and the pedestals of the others, evidently refer to something else, which, however, must be somehow connected with the Tiahuanaco year.

If the sculpture as depicted in Diagram 23 shows the solar year and its subdivision into convenient shorter periods, it would certainly appear logical to regard the symbols arranged round those heads in the form of 'haloes' as expressive of the *days*.

Each of the twelve heads is surrounded by twenty-four symbols. Altogether, therefore, there are $12 \times 24 = 288$ symbols. However, as two of the Twelfths evidently are meant to have óne additional symbol each (cf. Diagrams 17 and 18, on pp. 102 and 103) the full number of halo symbols is 290.

According to the Calendar on the Gateway of the Sun Temple of Kalasasaya the Tiahuanaco year, therefore, had 290 days.

The discussion and interpretation of the Calendar of Kalasasaya has been rather easy thus far. Now the difficulties begin with the question of the number of days in the Tiahuanaco year.

It is absolutely certain that only these $288 + 2 = 290$ halo-symbols have to be taken into consideration when establishing the number of days. There are another 157 symbols to be found in the 'solar year' part of the Calendar sculpture, but as they

100

are not in connexion with the 'month' haloes they obviously have no 'day' significance; besides, if we added them to the 290 halo-symbols the number would become too high, viz. 447, for it certainly would not do to take only part of them, i.e. as many as are necessary to make up a year of about 365 days, and to leave the rest.

The firmly established figure of 290 days does not allow any approximation at all to any existing or conceivable calendar system. As there are 290 days, and not 288, we cannot even speak of an arbitrary 'numerical' calendar based upon the conception '12 × 24', or '12(2 × 12)', or '12 × 12 + 12 × 12', which would go wandering over all the seasons, like the original Roman arbitrary 'year' of 'ten months', March to December, or as the year of the Julian Calendar was about to do before Gregory stepped in. Moreover, the Calendar *must* be a natural and an astronomical one because of its unmistakable balanced equinoxes and solstices. For the same reason it must be a *solar* one, and not, perhaps, a Venus Calendar, and it must cover the *whole* solar year.

Also the fact that the twelve heads have been given the significant shape of radiant suns serves as an additional strong pointer.

Here is where all attempts at interpretation have met with failure hitherto.

This being so we may offer with the more justification and confidence our own interpretation, which is based upon, and was inspired by, the teachings of Hoerbiger's Cosmological Theory of the terrestrial Satellites.

Before we proceed, let us visualize once more the exact state of things which obtained during the age of the girdle-tide. This is very important, for otherwise we are apt to forget that the Gregorian Calendar of Our Times and the Stone Calendar of Tiahuanaco are two absolutely different things.

Cosmic forces had caused the predecessor of our Moon to approach nearer and nearer to the Earth. As long as one

101

DIAGRAM 17
THE SIXTH TWELFTH ('AUGUST–SEPTEMBER')
featuring an additional day
Actual size.

DIAGRAM 18
THE EIGHTH TWELFTH ('OCTOBER-NOVEMBER')
featuring an additional day
Actual size.

revolution of the Satellite round the Earth (i.e. one real 'month') was longer than one day, the waters of the terrestrial oceans, held in thrall by the gravitational powers of the Satellite, and hence moving less quickly than the Earth rotated, acted like a band-brake. This eventually caused a considerable slowing up of the terrestrial rotation, and hence the length of the day grew.

According to Hoerbiger's Cosmological Theory, rotation results from the energy of the revolution of a satellite which is handed on to the primary during the last stages of the approach and the breakdown of the secondary. Hence that primeval accumulation of matter, the 'Proto-Earth', will have had no rotation at all. Each captured smaller accumulation of matter, —each approaching planeticle, planetlet, planet—however, set up tidal phenomena, and, whirling round ever faster in its approach, 'took along' the Earth and made it rotate. Finally, also, the rain of the satellitic material which hit the Earth after the disintegration of each satellite urged on the terrestrial rotation. Thus the Earth got its present speed of rotation chiefly through the accelerating action of the predecessor of our present Moon. Hence it must have rotated appreciably more slowly before it was thus speeded up. Luna, our present Satellite, tries to retard again the terrestrial rotation. In the course of its Aeon it will cause an appreciable lengthening of the day, measured in hours of present length. Only in the last stages of its existence will it speed up the rotation of our Earth, even to considerably less than 24 hours of present length.

In 1927, when investigating certain problems relating to terrestrial rotation, Hans Hoerbiger came to the conclusion that at the remote time when the predecessor of our present Moon was captured out of transterrestrial space, the Earth may have taken something like 27 hours of present length to swing once completely round. During the age of the approach of that Satellite, the Earth's rotation was slowed down till the day had a length of about 30 hours. This stage was reached at the 'Stationary Period', when 'day' and 'month', i.e. terrestrial rotation and satellitic revolution, were equal in length. After this period the Satellite moved more quickly round the Earth than our planet rotated: hence it 'took along' the Earth and accelerated its rotation. In the final cataclysm the present speed of terrestrial rotation was reached, equal to 24 hours, now really such of 'present length'.

One of Hoerbiger's calculations showed that when the distance between the centre of the Satellite and the centre of the Earth was 5·9 terrestrial radii, the 'day' had had to decrease from its maximum of 30 hours to 29·4 hours, while the 'month' then was only 19·6 hours long. Nine 'months', therefore, were equal to six 'days'.[53]

While the 'day' of the time when the Satellite's centre was only 5·9 terrestrial radii from the Earth's centre was longer than it is now, because the age-long post-stationary onward urge had not yet had its full effect on the terrestrial rotation, and the final breakdown acceleration had not yet happened, the *year* was practically of the same length as now, as the resistance of the interplanetary medium has not had any really considerable effect on the period of the terrestrial orbital revolution during—say—the last five hundred thousand years. The difference, even if this speeding up should have amounted to an hour or two, is too slight to have to be taken into calculation, and would not materially affect the result. We may, therefore, accept the length of the year of that time as having been 8766 hours, as now. As, according to Hans Hoerbiger's computations, the day's length was then 29·4 of our present hours, the year of that time had not 365¼ days, but only 298 days. As regards the lunations, or real months, of which we now have not quite thirteen per year, there were 447 per year at the time when the centre to centre distance between the Earth and the Satellite was 5·9 terrestrial radii.

We may now attempt to answer the Questions put on pp. 90 and 91.

1. The Solar Year—that is, the time taken by the Earth to

complete one revolution round the Sun—is not always of the
same length. Owing to the resistance of the interplanetary
medium, the terrestrial orbit is a fine inward-tending spiral.
Hence the 'year' was the longer the further we go back in the
life-history of our Earth. It will decrease more and more in the
future, and will become shorter even than Mercury's present
year of 88 days, till the Earth, having spiralled quite close to
the Sun, will eventually disintegrate and its material will become united with the Sun's, speeding on the solar rotation
through its downrush. However, for the time under consideration, even though it may amount to several hundred thousand
years, the diminution of the Earth's orbit is a factor so slight
as to be negligible for all practical intents and purposes. We
may, therefore, consider that towards the end of the Tertiary
Age the solar year was as long as it is now: 8766 hours of present length (instead of, perhaps, 8767 or 8768 hours).

2. According to Hoerbiger's calculations, the solar year had
fewer days then, because the Earth rotated more slowly and
the day's length was consequently greater. Hoerbiger computed that the year may have had 298 days of 29·4 hours of
present length at that period of our Earth's history.

3. The division of the Year of Tiahuanaco into twelve parts
was evidently suggested by certain—compelling—astronomical aspects then obtaining, for it is difficult to suppose that this
duodecimal notation is a mere arbitrary feature. The 'twelfths'
of the Tiahuanaco year had no lunar significance, and could not
have had any, under the circumstances obtaining then.
Contrary to our own calendar, the days of the Tiahuanaco
Calendar were evenly distributed. The number of days in each
Twelfth has been clearly indicated by the sculptor.

4. The deviser of the Stone Calendar did show all the 447
real revolutions of the satellite which occurred in one solar
year at that time. He also showed, separately, the number of
real revolutions per Twelfth. Furthermore, he noted the
apparent revolutions per year, and the apparent revolutions of
the satellite per Twelfth.

THE CALENDAR OF KALASASAYA

According to Edmund Kiss, who unravelled most of the problems of the Stone Calendar on the monolithic gateway of the Sun Temple of Kalasasaya in Tiahuanaco, we may accept the 290 days represented by the symbols of the haloes round the twelve heads as the correct number to reckon with. They represent the solar year of that time. This had practically the same number of hours as the solar year of our time, i.e. 8766 hours of present length. However, as at the time when the Calendar was devised the Satellite had not yet, through its control over the girdle-tide, urged on the rotation of the Earth to its present speed, i.e. 24 hours of present length, the days must have been longer. Their length was, according to the Calendar, $8766 \div 290 = 30 \cdot 2$ hours of present length. This figure will alter only very slightly if the year was longer at that time, say 8767 hours, or so.

If we compare the findings of Edmund Kiss in 1929 and 1937 with the calculations Hoerbiger made in 1927 ('Stage 24' of his 'Table No. 533', filed in the Archives of the Hoerbiger Institute in Vienna) we find that the Austrian cosmologist— who did not know, and could not have known, anything about the meaning of the Stone Calendar, but had based his calculations solely upon the theorems of his own Cosmological Theory, which in its turn is founded upon technological considerations— had determined the time of rotation of our Earth at the age when the centre to centre distance of the Earth and Satellite was $5 \cdot 9$ Earth radii, as having been about $29 \cdot 4$ hours of present length, while according to the Calendar of Tiahuanaco, the Earth then took $30 \cdot 2$ hours of present length to rotate. The difference between the two figures amounts to only $2\frac{1}{2}\%$. Hoerbiger's figure is therefore a most remarkable result of reasoning and reckoning, and the figure revealed by the Stone Calendar gives a fine proof of the correctness of his leading idea. This proof is so much the more valuable in that it comes from an unexpected quarter.

However, as the writer has repeatedly found in his experience, Hoerbiger's Theory is expected by its opponents to give answers of one hundred per cent. exactitude, even to questions where it is alone in the field with a solution. The difference between the length of the day as revealed by the Stone Calendar and the length of the day as calculated by Hoerbiger is due to the fact that the Viennese scientist had to use figures and formulae which, unlike other makers of hypotheses, he did not find printed in any book of reference, but which he had to evolve for himself. Such an undertaking is not easy, and its results have generally to be modified by successive generations of investigators—as has been the case with all similar calculations hitherto. Hoerbiger died in 1931, while Kiss published his first article in the German magazine, *Der Schluessel*, in 1934, further results in 1936, and his final decipherment, in book-form, only in 1937. Hoerbiger's followers might therefore take the hint given by the Stone Calendar with such authoritative distinctness and directness, and either accept a slower original rotatory speed of the Earth, or attribute less power (i.e. smaller size and/or mass, and hence also urging on tidal grip) to the former Satellite, whose actual mass, of course, must remain a matter of speculation. But the adherents of the Satellitic Theory consider Hoerbiger's theoretical figure near enough to the actual figure revealed by the Stone Calendar to be satisfactory to all intents and purposes, and they hence abstain from 'doctoring' the original calculations.

The Symbols

Before we proceed with our description and analysis of the Calendar of Tiahuanaco, and to the discussion and interpretation of its notation, it may be helpful and interesting to pass in review the different symbols which the deviser and designer of the sculptured time-chart employed.

Even a superficial survey shows that the symbols fall into two groups which are sharply differentiated as to form—and hence, we may presume, also as to meaning.

The symbols of the first group we may call the *Numerical Symbols*. Of these there are altogether 1107 and they show 24

108

different forms which, with two notable exceptions, are taken from the animal kingdom.[54] 447 of these symbols are found on the 'solar year part' of the Calendar, the remaining 660 are attached to the thirty winged figures which are arranged in the two 'panels' on either side of the dominating central figure. 290 of the 447 symbols just mentioned constitute the twelve 'haloes', which make up the 'solar year' of Tiahuanaco proper; 157 are not so attached: 38, for instance, evidently constituting a definite group, appear on the 'body' of the central figure; 13, obviously constituting another group, are on the pedestal of the First Twelfth; the remaining 106 are 'scattered' over the whole 'solar year' part of the Calendar, and are therefore evidently not to be regarded as a special grouping, but only as part of that total of 157 symbols. It should be clearly understood that whatever 'symbolic' or 'determinative' meaning these 'numerical' symbols may also have, they are primarily *'counters'*, each one, irrespective of its form or size, denoting the same—namely: 'One Unit'. Unlike the Mayas, therefore, the Tiahuanacans were able to express numbers only by stringing the requisite amount of units together.

The second group of symbols consists of 'geometrical' designs, of seven different forms. From their abstract form alone we may infer that these designs are not meant to be 'symbols' in the above sense at all. We therefore call them the *'Non-Numerical Symbols'*. Some of them seem to have a 'determinative', or 'operational', meaning—operational in the sense of arithmetical operations. Two of the second group of symbols are certainly merely ornamental.

FIRST GROUP: NUMERICAL SYMBOLS
First Series: Satellitic Symbols

Symbol 1. *Disk.* This is the most frequent of all symbols which are descriptive of the Satellite, and, indeed, of all

symbols. It is exclusively used in the haloes, that is, as a *day* symbol, and never occurs among the 157 other symbols of the solar year part of the Calendar. In the haloes it occupies the 2nd, 3rd, 5th, 6th, 8th, 9th, 11th, 12th, 14th, 15th, 17th, 18th, 20th, 21st, 23rd, and 24th, positions and occurs altogether 192 times. It is also used 50 times on the winged lateral figures.

The Disk has not to be counted in all cases where it is obviously used only as a *determinative* (the 'nose' of the toxodons [cf. Symbol 21] and pumas [cf. Symbols 3 and 4]), or as an *ornament* (in condor and puma 'crowns' [cf. Symbols 4 and 17]). It goes without saying that eyes, additional eyes (cf. face of the central figure), ears, nostrils, and similar round forms, also do not count as 'disks'.[55]

Symbol 2. *Elongated Disk*. A special form of Symbol 1. Used 12 times, in haloes only, and always as the 13th symbol. As will be shown later, the thirteenth day was the only day in each Twelfth on which the satellite both rose and set in the course of one day. The satellite, so to speak, 'extended' over all the day: hence this 'elongated' form is attributed to the satellitic disk-symbol.

The unique, *bracket-like*, 'support' of the elongated disk-symbol seems to have been specially employed to stress this 'extension'.

Symbol 3. *Plain Puma's Head*. Used as a halo symbol only in the halo of the First Twelfth, where it appears six times, instead of the toxodon's head, in the 4th, 10th, 16th, and 22nd, positions, and instead of the plain condor's head in the 7th and 19th positions. Eight more plain puma's heads are depicted on the body of the First Twelfth, and 14 appear on, or in, the

110

pedestals of the First, Fifth, Sixth, Seventh, Eighth, and Ninth Twelfths. Altogether there are 28 plain puma's heads on the sculpture.[56]

Symbol 4. *Crowned Puma's Head.* Occurs only twice : at either end of the pedestal of the First Twelfth. (Further remarks on p. 121.)

Symbol 5. *Puma's Face.* Used only in the First Twelfth: seven times on its body, and once in its pedestal.

Symbol 6. *Plumed Puma's Face.* Occurs only once: as the 'first' symbol in the halo of the First, or Autumn Equinox, Twelfth. (Cf. also Symbols 7 and 8.) The peculiar 'plume' (of 'condor's feathers') is depicted as if emanating from behind the puma's face. The symbol is really a sort of composite satellitic-solar one, and the idea expressed is: The Day of a Special Eclipse of the Sun by the Satellite, which determined the beginning of the First, and of each, Twelfth. The 'plume' represents a sheaf of solar corona rays and is therefore characterized by 'condor's feathers'. (Further remarks on pp. 141 foll.)

Symbol 7. Same symbol as 6, with the puma's face 'abbreviated', because of the small space available. Used only once, as the 'first' symbol of the halo of the Seventh, or Spring Equinox, Twelfth. (Cf. Diagram 14.)

111

Symbol 8. Same symbol as 6 and 7, with the puma's face 'abbreviated' out of existence. Employed as the 'first' symbol of

the haloes of the remaining ten Twelfths. This, or a similar, symbol is also used, as a mere ornament, with no separate numerical sense, in the 'crowns' of Symbols 4 and 17, and in the peculiar headgear of the two Solstice Trumpeters. (Cf. Diagrams 15 and 16.)

Symbol 9. *Fish's Head*. Fish's heads occur as additional symbols in the Third, Fifth, Ninth, and Eleventh Twelfths, altogether 14 times. The special meaning of the use of this symbol there is unknown. The peculiar almost vertical mouth of the fishes is a characteristic which the Orestias of Lake Titicaca still show. The fish's head is pre-eminently employed on the lateral winged figures, where it occurs altogether 240 times.

Symbol 10. *Flying Fish*. A surprising symbol indicating beyond any doubt that at the time when Tiahuanaco flourished it must have had a tropical climate. It is used twice only, as an 'additional' symbol in the haloes of the Sixth and Eighth Twelfths, to show that these had not 24, but 25 days. (Cf. Diagrams 17 and 18.)

The flying fish symbol is attached to the left 'cheek' of the head of the Sixth Twelfth, and to the right one of the Eighth Twelfth. This appears at first sight to be due merely to symmetry of design. However, on thorough analysis, this is found to be fortuitous, for the position of the symbols (or, rather, of the 'additional' days they stand for) is determined by astronomical necessity. (Cf. pp. 148f.)

112

Symbol 11. *Abbreviated Flying Fish.* Used only once: at the upper end of the stave which the figure of the First Twelfth

holds in its right hand. (Cf. pp. 124 foll.)

Symbol 12. *Fish's Tail.* Used only once in the solar year part of the calendar sculpture: at the end of a peculiar 'fish'-like shape on the body of the First Twelfth. Its meaning there is evidently: 'end' of that which was started by the head of the puma-faced 'fish'-shape. (Cf. Note 64.) This symbol also occurs in the 'crowns' of the lateral winged figures, always as the fifth, and last, 'jewel', altogether 30 times. (Cf. Diagram 20.)

Symbol 13. *Human Face.* Used only twice, as a sort of maniple at the elbows of the figure of the First Twelfth.

Symbol 14. *Human Head.* Used only twice: grasped, like a trophy, in the hands of the Solstice Trumpeters. (Cf. Diagrams 15 and 16.)

Altogether there are 276 Satellitic Symbols among the 447 symbols on the Calendar. 224 of them are found in the haloes, that is, they refer to something in the solar year part.

Second Series: Solar Symbols

Symbol 15. *Plain Condor's Head.* Always appears in the haloes as the 7th and 19th symbol—except in the First Twelfth, where it is replaced by puma's heads at these positions—altogether 22 times. It is also used 17 times on the body of the

First Twelfth, and 64 times in the great meander, and on, or in, the pedestals. The grand total of plain condor's heads is 103. On the lateral winged figures 260 plain condor's heads are used.

Symbol 16. *Crested Condor's Head.* Occurs only twice: at the lower ends of the staves which the figure of the First Twelfth holds in its hands.

(It may be that this symbol, as well as the following one, depicts the *male* condor, whose head actually bears a fleshy 'comb'. If so, Symbol 15 may depict the female.)

Symbol 17. *Crowned Condor's Head.* This is also used only twice: at either end of the great meander which determines the proper succession of the Twelfths, and hence the course of the solar year. (Cf. p. 95.)

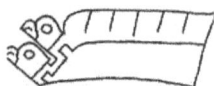

Symbol 18. *Mating Condor.* Occurs only twice (in pairs, in characteristic attitude), as a sort of determinative symbol, in the Second and Twelfth Twelfths. The 'male' and the 'female' have to be counted as separate numerical symbols. Special meaning unknown, but perhaps relating to the main mating times of the condors.

The fact that both these pairs of condors look towards the *left*, and not, as would be in accordance with symmetry (cf. Symbol 10), one pair of them to the right, must be evaluated as a 'pointer', or 'reading help', showing in which direction one is to proceed in counting the heads.

Symbol 19. *'Sitting' Condor*. Occurs only twice, as a sort of determinative symbol, in the Sixth and Eighth Twelfths. The condor, whose head must be supposed hidden under a wing, is depicted as sitting on five 'eggs' (Symbol 20). Special meaning unknown, but perhaps relating to the main nesting times of the condors.

Symbol 20. *Condor's Egg*. Occurs only under the 'sitting' condors in the Sixth and Eighth Twelfths, in clutches of five. This symbol is not to be confused with the Non-Numerical Symbol 7, which is of similar form. (May I be forgiven for presenting 'eggs' of so unorthodox a shape. Their apparently excessive number—at present the condor lays only two—need not be objected to, as obviously no 'zoological' reference is attempted here.)

Symbol 21. *Toxodon's Head*. Used chiefly in the haloes, in the 4th, 10th, 16th, and 22nd, positions (except in the halo of the First Twelfth, where puma's heads appear there), altogether 44 times. Another four toxodons are used: two each on either of the Solstice Trumpeters. (See also Note 56.) 20 more toxodon's heads appear on the winged lateral figures.

Altogether there are 171 Solar Symbols among the 447 symbols on the Calendar.

Third Series: Symbols used exclusively in the Winged Lateral Figures

Symbol 22. *Crayfish*. Occurs only as an eye-appendage of the ten condor-headed lateral figures. (10 times.) Satellitic symbol.

Symbol 23. *Wing-tip*. Occurs only as an eye-appendage of the ten condor-headed lateral figures and of the ten anthropoid figures of the lowest row. (20 times.) Solar symbol.

Symbol 24. *'Snail' Shell*. Occurs only as the second 'jewel' in the 'crowns' of the thirty lateral figures. (30 times.) Solar Symbol.

The reason why the satellitic symbols are much more diversified in form than the solar ones is probably due to the fact that the Satellite had many different phases and aspects.

SECOND GROUP: NON-NUMERICAL SYMBOLS

Symbols 1, 2, and 3, are evidently closely related, and probably denote 'graduations' of whatever they express. It would appear to me as if the sculptor had tried to depict 'knots' of different complicacy. Arrangements of knots, *quipus*, were indeed used at a later time in this region for recording certain facts. (The origin of the system is unknown but may well be very ancient.) Moreover, 'tying' (and 'untying') may easily have some chronographic meaning.

Symbol. 1. *Single Knot*. Occurs only twice: in the pedestals of the Third and Eleventh Twelfths. It would therefore seem

that these two Twelfths had something in common—what, has not yet been ascertained. May mean 'once', or 'single', or 'plus one'.

Symbol 2. *Double Knot*. Occurs 46 times: once in the centre of the body of the First Twelfth, four times on the 'braces' of the same figure, once in the pedestal of the Seventh Twelfth, 10 times on the bodies of the ornithoid lateral winged figures, and 30 times on the objects which all the lateral winged figures hold in their hands. May express the idea 'twice', or 'double', 'two together', or 'plus two'.

25 of these 46 'double knots' seem to be definitely used with the meaning of 'tying two units into a pair': the four symbols on the 'braces' of the figure of the First Twelfth and the one in the centre of its body (cf. also p. 146), which tie up pairs of condors; and 20 on the objects which the lateral winged figures of the first and second row carry (pairs of fishes).

The 'double knot' which forms a sort of pedestal in the centre of the body of the First Twelfth, and that in the pedestal of the Seventh Twelfth, evidently show that these two Twelfths have something in common—what, still needs finding.

Symbol 3. *Treble Knot*. Occurs only twice: on the pedestals of the Sixth and Eighth Twelfths. These two Twelfths are thus

117

somehow linked, but the reason why is not yet clear. However, it is certainly significant that the *treble* knots' should be used in the two Twelfths which contain 25 days. (Reference to additional eclipses or passages of the Satellite?) May denote 'thrice', or 'treble', or 'plus three'.

Symbol 4. '*Canceller.*' This symbol, whose form somehow suggests to me 'movement' (cf. Symbol 6), or 'untying', occurs 24 times: four times in the pedestals of the Second, Fifth, Ninth, and Twelfth Twelfths, and 20 times on the bodies of the anthropoid lateral winged figures. What the four Twelfths mentioned have in common has not yet transpired in the analysis. May be employed as a 'diminisher', meaning 'minus' (*sc.* one).

It might be mentioned here that the Fourth and Tenth Twelfths do not show any of the above-mentioned symbols, but are 'natural'. Whatever may be expressed by these symbols, therefore, did not obtain in the solstitial Twelfths.

Symbol 5. *Fraction Indicator*. Ostensibly a semicircle, it is used once only, in the First Twelfth, to express the quantity of 'one half' (cf. p. 126).

Symbol 6. Meanderlike ornament which surrounds the 'heads' and supports the Day Symbols. Similar in form to Symbol 4, and perhaps meaning 'movement', or 'progress' (of time). This meander-band somehow gives me the impression that it is 'moving' counter-clockwise. As we know, this is actually the direction in which all symbols on the Calendar are supposed to be read. The number of the elements, 18 round the head of the First Twelfth and 8 round each of the eleven others, is probably of no significance. There are also twice two similar elements on the shoulders, or arms, of the figure of the First Twelfth. (Mistakes in the drawing of these meander-bands have been pointed out at their proper places.)

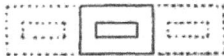

Symbol 7. Ornamental element, similar to Numerical Symbol 20, apparently only used to relieve ribbon-like parts—as, for instance, on the 'staves' and the 'girdle' of the figure of the First Twelfth, as well as in the 'crests' and 'crowns' of Symbols 4, 16, and 17, and in the 'crowns' and on the 'cloaks' of the lateral winged figures, and on the 'staves' of the lowest row of these figures.

The wing-like arrangements surrounding the eyes of the faces in full view and in profile are probably symbolic of the 'flight of time'.

The Notation of the Movements of the Former Satellite

It may be objected that the similarity between the number of days of the solar year at the time of Tiahuanaco as calculated by Hoerbiger and that shown on the Calendar Gate is merely a coincidence. We shall therefore quote another fact which will suffice to remove this accusation and serve to secure our platform.

We shall try to see whether the Calendar on the monolithic temple gate of Tiahuanaco also shows the 'months', that is, the real and/or apparent revolutions of the Satellite round the Earth. Hoerbiger calculated the length of the 'month' at a distance of the centre of the Satellite from the Earth's centre of 5·9 terrestrial radii, as 19·6 hours of present length, so that in one year the Satellite performed 'really'—that is, as seen by an

119

extra-terrestrial observer—447 revolutions round our planet. 'Apparently'—that is, as seen by an observer on the Earth— the Satellite performed only 157 revolutions in one year. This was due to the difference between the speed of the Earth's rotation and the Satellite's orbital motion. If the 'real' and/or 'apparent' revolutions are shown at all, the one or the other of these numbers, or both, must appear in the Stone Calendar.

Our own calendars also give indications as to the actual lunations by printing little bright or dark disks, and little crescents open towards the left or the right, to show whether the Moon is full or new, or waxing or waning. The knowledge as to the date of the lunar phases is of no importance whatever to the average man; the indications are given for the sake of completeness and for the convenience of those few who may need them: for instance, people who want to check up on the date of Easter, who have to drive a car at night, or who want to make a moonlight ramble. We may therefore suppose that at the time of the making of the Tiahuanaco Calendar also, the indication of the number of real and apparent revolutions was not very important. Nevertheless both the number of the real and of the apparent revolutions was recorded, for the sake of completeness and for the use of those few who might have had need of them. The record is certainly of great value for us.

From the point of view of the present book the number of the revolutions of the Satellite may one day prove a valuable indicator regarding the 'date' of the calendar sculpture, and hence also of the Classic Tiahuanaco Culture. At present we can only calculate the distance of the centre of the Satellite from the centre of the Earth at that time—5·9 terrestrial radii. As we can see no way so far to translate this physical fact into terms of time, the reference as it stands cannot be regarded yet as a 'time basis'.

The number of satellitic revolutions *per year* would, logically, have to appear marked on the *year* part of the Calendar. The deviser of the calendar has done so, indeed, but as the inclusion of the requisite number of symbols to denote the

120

satellitic revolutions would have greatly overladen the 'heads' and crowded into insignificance the much more important notation of the days, he has decided to make the day symbols do duty also as symbols for the revolution of the Satellite.

An ingenious system of 'pointers' helps the beholder to figure out the number of satellitic revolutions.

The figure of the First Twelfth stands on a peculiar pedestal in which, and on which, a number of significant symbols are to be found (cf. Diagram 19). In the very centre of the pedestal we notice a puma-faced 'fish',[57] bent double. It is 'contained' in a 'box' which is connected by means of a system of lines with six condor heads and four puma heads. This symbolism is in its turn enclosed in the meandroid step-motif which forms the pedestal, at whose right and left ends two crowned puma heads take up commanding positions.

These two crowned puma heads are important 'pointers'. Just as the similarly placed heads of the *Kunturi Mayku*, the 'Condor Paramount-Chief', at the ends of the great meander-line told us that what they 'contain' is something with reference to the Sun, the *number of days* of the Solar Year, the two heads of the *Titi Mayku*, the 'Puma Paramount-Chief', personifications of the Satellite, want to tell us that they 'contain' something worth knowing about the Satellite. The most interesting information would be the *number of satellitic revolutions* in the same spell of time.

Whatever else the *twelve* symbols of the central pedestal—six puma heads and six condor heads—may be intended to express, in the present instance they are evidently to be evaluated as an 'abbreviated' reference, or 'pointer', to the *twelve* 'heads' of the Solar Year, with their 290 symbols.

That our surmise is correct can be checked from the end-ornaments of the pedestals upon which the eleven heads rest and the full figure stands (cf. Diagram 23): six of them feature pumas and four condors; two of them—the solstice Twelfths—have no pedestals because otherwise the trumpeters would have become too diminutive: but as each of these figures stands

121

directly on the condor-adorned great meander, which, so to speak, forms their pedestal, these two Twelfths can with every justice be added to those determined by condor-pedestals.

The puma-faced 'fish' is a double symbol for the Satellite, the 'Terrible One' which also holds sway over the 'Waters'. The puma-fish determines the meaning of the twelve symbols surrounding it: they refer to the solar year (viz. the 290 day symbols), but only in so far as it can be brought into relation with the Satellite. The 'all-comprising' meandroid step-motif of the pedestal finally urges the beholder to augment this number by adding *all* the remaining symbols to be found on the Calendar sculpture which are connected by the great meander and which, not being in direct connexion with the heads, cannot have reference to days. The number thus resulting would refer to the one thing worth recording with regard to the Satellite itself: the number of its revolutions per year.

If we follow these directions and count out all the numerical symbols on the solar year part of the Calendar (Diagram 23) we get, besides the

290 day symbols in connexion with the haloes, 157 others, consisting of:

38 extra symbols (condors, pumas, etc.) on the body of the figure of the First Twelfth;

13 symbols on and in the pedestal of the figure of the First Twelfth; and

106 extra symbols (condors, pumas, fishes, etc.) in the line of the eleven Twelfths, which are not in connexion with the haloes; altogether, therefore:

447 symbols.

This total says that at the period when the Calendar of Tiahuanaco was devised the Satellite revolved 447 times round the Earth in one year. Accepting the length of the Solar Year to have been 8766 hours of present length, the Satellite, therefore, took 19·6 hours of present length to revolve once round the Earth.

The distinctly separate sub-total of 157 symbols which are not contained in the 'year part' of the Calendar, refer to the 157 'apparent revolutions' of the Satellite observable from the Earth. The Satellite took 55·9 hours of present length to perform one of these apparent revolutions.

If we now compare Kiss's result of investigations of 1934 with Hoerbiger's result of calculation of 1927, we find complete correspondence. That the calculated number of revolutions coincides with the result of observation recorded in the Calendar sculpture is due to the fact that at the time when the centre to centre distance of the Earth and the Satellite was 5·9 terrestrial radii, and when, incidentally, the Satellite-controlled girdle-tide had reached the level of Tiahuanaco, the Satellite was forced by the physical laws of orbital motion to move round the Earth 447 times in one year, or once every 19·6 hours of present length. On the other hand, the small difference of $2\frac{1}{2}$ per cent. between the calculated day's length and the day's length as revealed by the Calendar, is due to the fact that Hoerbiger had somewhat over-estimated the onward urge which the friction of the faster-moving tidal ring would impart to the Earth, and had also believed that the Earth had rotated somewhat more quickly in earlier times than evidently it had.

Let us now investigate another question: Does the Calendar of Kalasasaya also show how many revolutions there were in each Twelfth? A calculation shows that the Satellite revolved practically exactly 37 times round the Earth in each Twelfth of 24 days.

As the number of satellitic revolutions per year was shown spread all over the sculpture expressive of the year, we should logically look to find the number of revolutions per Twelfth spread over *one* at least of the Twelfths. For one example would suffice, and be valid for the other Twelfths, too. The number of revolutions per Twelfth would probably be shown in a prominent place so that it could be easily seen and readily ascertained. The best place, and the only one allowing the distinct display of a sufficient number of additional symbols, would be the figure of the First Twelfth. This is actually the place the maker of the Calendar has chosen, and for this reason alone he has added a 'body' to the first 'head'. (Cf. Diagram 19.)

To leave no doubt that the body of the First Twelfth has to be considered by itself and apart from the head, and that, contrary to the 'solar' meaning of the latter, it referred to the Satellite, the deviser of the Calendar has furnished the beholder with another unmistakable 'pointer'. It is another crescent-shaped 'puma-faced fish', already familiar to us as symbolizing the Satellite; it too is made up of neutral ornamental elements, and is shown, on an 'abbreviated' pedestal, in the centre of the body of the figure of the First Twelfth. (Cf. also p. 143 for another 'pointer' evaluation of this symbol.) This pointer suggests: 'To find the number of revolutions of the Satellite in this, and hence in each, Twelfth, count all the symbols on the body of this figure.' When doing so we find 38 symbols.

At first sight it looks as if the deviser of the Calendar had slipped up here and carved one symbol too many—but on closer analysis it becomes evident that the total of 38 is not meant to apply in all cases. The actual total given is only 37, but in two cases this figure is to be exceeded. The sculptor himself draws our attention to this fact by means of an unmistakable 'reading help'.

Conspicuously placed as the first symbol at the top left[58] we see a 'flying fish', a symbol which we have evaluated as meaning 'one more', in the Sixth and Eighth Twelfths. It is only in reference to these 'augmented Twelfths' that the flying fish at the top left applies. In these, which had 25 days instead of 24, the Satellite must have revolved about $38\frac{1}{2}$ times round the Earth. As it is obviously difficult, if not impossible, to express a fraction by the method of notation of units employed by the sculptor of the Stone Calendar of Tiahuanaco we would not judge him too hardly if he had chosen to 'neglect' this fraction. As a matter of fact it appears that he has faithfully

124

DIAGRAM 19. THE FIRST TWELFTH

or Twelfth of the Autumnal Equinox ('March–April') and its Pedestal.

(The symbols picked out in red show the number of real revolutions of the Satellite per Twelfth. The 13 symbols on the pedestal denote its apparent revolutions in the same period.)

125

recorded it. For at the side of this flying fish at the top left we notice a peculiar 'non-numerical' geometrical symbol: a semi-circle. This, if it means anything at all, can only express the idea: 'one half' (or 'part of one'). And thus we get the total of $38\frac{1}{2}$ for the number of satellitic revolutions in the Flying Fish Twelfths. (Cf. again Diagram 19 where the symbols referring to the numbers of revolutions of the Satellite per Twelfth have been picked out in red.)

The 13 symbols on the pedestal of the First Twelfth must be taken to allude to the 13 'apparent revolutions', which were observable by every Tiahuanacan in each Twelfth.

Before we conclude the discussion of the problems of the Tiahuanaco Calendar it may be worth while to ponder over the question whether the symbols employed for expressing the days have been chosen only with a view to divide the ring of day-counters into convenient small groups, to facilitate the counting—or whether they have been used also for some other, more important reason. While the former endeavour seems obvious, the symbols certainly appear also to refer to conditions obtaining at the time when the sculpture was made. The most interesting reference, for instance, might be to eclipses.

Both the Sun and the Satellite were, of course, capable of being eclipsed. As the eclipses of the latter must have been, then as now, long-drawn-out affairs without a very clearly defined beginning and end the solar eclipses alone will have been of interest, then as now. Because of the nearness of the Satellite and its large apparent size every one of its 447 annual revolutions must have produced an impressive total solar eclipse in the tropical girdle (and, of course, a similar number of—uninteresting—eclipses of the Satellite). Half of these would be visible for any terrestrial observer, the other half would happen below his horizon. Let us now investigate whether the Calendar of Kalasasaya actually contains references to the number of eclipses.

126

An analysis of the halo symbols shows that these consist of two distinctly different—and, in fact, antagonistic—groups:

Disks (Symbol 1)	192
Elongated Disks (Symbol 2)	12
Puma faces with rays (Symbols 6, 7, 8)	12
Puma heads (Symbol 5)	6
Flying Fishes (Symbol 10)	2
Total of satellitic symbols	224
Toxodon heads (Symbol 21)	44
Condor heads (Symbol 15)	22
Total of solar symbols	66
Total of halo symbols	290

The above figure of 224 satellitic symbols expresses the number of total eclipses of the Sun; on these days the Satellite was 'predominant': they were 'Satellite Days'. On the remaining 66 days of the year no solar eclipse was observable at Tiahuanaco: hence they were noted as 'Sun Days'.

It goes without saying that the exact rhythm of the eclipses will not have strictly followed the pattern of satellitic and solar symbols in the haloes; but this is a minor matter. The important thing is that the *total* of possible solar eclipses is correctly shown.

Let us now investigate the problem of the notation of total solar eclipses per Twelfth.

The halo of the First Twelfth is arranged differently from the haloes of the other eleven. Instead of a continuous ring we see the symbols distinctly arranged into two lots: 19 + 5. While these five symbols are always satellitic ones the 19 others are exclusively characteristic of the Satellite only in the halo of the First Twelfth. Evidently we are thus to be reminded that here something interesting about the Satellite is told. The idea suggested is: The Satellite is preponderant, that is, causing solar eclipses, nineteen times per Twelfth.

This number is repeated once more on the *body* of the First

Twelfth where—as if in order to make doubly sure—the sculptor also gives what may be interpreted as a reference to the number of satellitic eclipses, that is, the occasions when the Sun beat the Satellite. If we arrange the 38 symbols on the body of the First Twelfth into a satellitic and a solar group we find that there are 19 symbols in either: 8 puma heads, 7 puma faces, 2 'human' heads, 1 fish tail, and 1 flying fish, on the one hand, and on the other 19 condor heads.

It may be objected that a total of 19 eclipses is a little too high per ordinary twelfth and slightly too low per augmented twelfth. It may be that in the first case the 'decapitated' form of the flying fish and in the second the 'semicircle' give warning that fractions, minus or plus, are involved here.

The Winged Figures

The sculpture on the Gate also shows thirty winged symbolic figures above the long bottom line of the Calendar, a panel of fifteen on either side of the figure of the First Twelfth, arranged in three rows of five each.[59] (Only the first figures of the three rows of five to the right of the figure of the First Twelfth are shown in Diagram 20. Those on the left are practically exact counterparts, the chief difference being that they face towards the right.) The space occupied by these twice fifteen winged figures can be seen on Diagram 12. Each of these 30 winged figures bears 22 symbols, that is 660 altogether. These 660 symbols fall into two distinct groups of 330 each, one of which is 'solar', and the other 'satellitic'; or, viewed from another angle: one refers to the 'day', and one to the 'night'. Significantly, the two major numbers of either group of symbols total up to 290. There are: 260 condor heads and 30 shells (whose spiral structure points to the solar path), plus 20 wing-tips and 20 toxodon heads; and 240 fish heads and 50 disks, plus 30 fish tails and 10 crayfish. Another interesting, and evidently also significant, point is that the solar and satellitic symbols on the figures are distributed very unequally: the twenty anthropoid figures bear 130 satellitic symbols and

128

DIAGRAM 20

The anthropoid and ornithoid winged lateral figures

Only the first of each row of five of the panel to the right of the First Twelfth and its pedestal is shown in this diagram, the others being identical. The figures of the panel of three times five to the left of the First Twelfth face towards the right. (Scale in inches.)

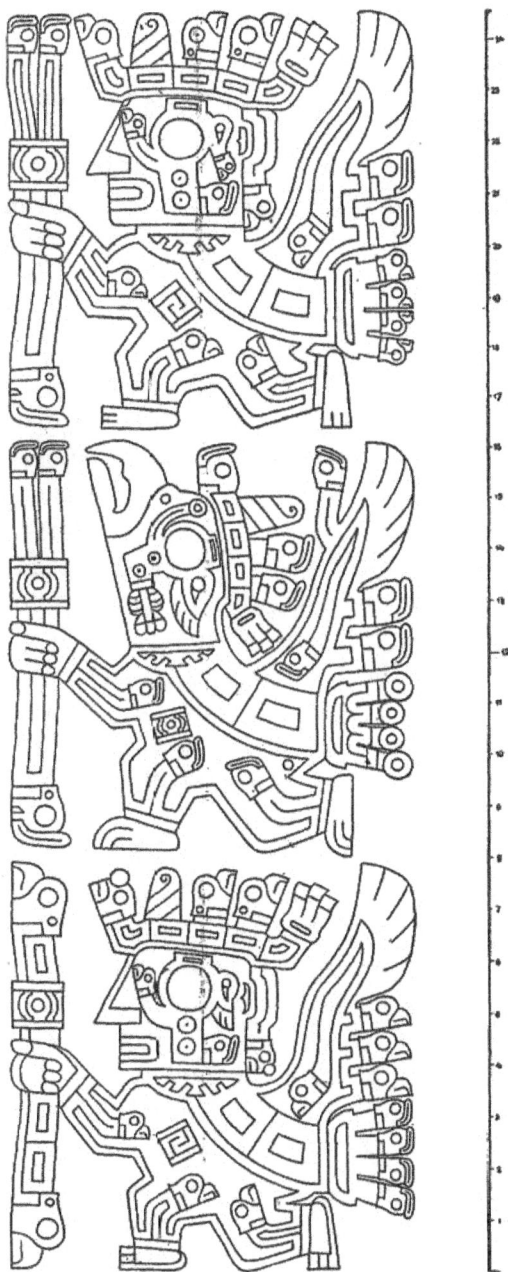

310 solar ones, while the ten condor figures show 200 satellitic symbols and only 20 solar ones. Obviously something important with regard to the Satellite is being stressed in this way. (Cf. Note 71.)

As the anthropoid and ornithoid figures are not connected by meanders, or in any other obvious immediate way, with the solar year part of the Calendar, they cannot refer to it directly; on the other hand, as they are present on that monument of chronological notation they must be connected somehow with the calculation, or notation, of time.

The anthropoid and ornithoid figures are depicted in violent motion: their wings beating, their feet running. If they denote 'time' at all, then they must denote 'swiftly moving, quickly passing time'. As the year, the twelfths, and the days, have been shown already, the only reference to the division of time which might yet be depicted, would be one to 'hours'. The number of the figures, thirty, does not speak against this view, and the running, flying shape of the figures even supports it. The Tiahuanacans, therefore, may have divided their 'day' (of 30·2 hours of present length) into 30 'hours' (each 1 hour and 24 seconds of present time in length.)

The twenty-two symbols which each figure carries may be indicative of 'minutes'.

This is the interpretation which Edmund Kiss, very diffidently, puts forward. He evidently boggles at the idea of a 'clock' being depicted here, and also seems to be unhappy about the number of the 'hours', thirty. Yet, as will be shown later, Kiss's general idea is quite right. Let me stress here that not a 'clock' is depicted in these panels, but a table showing the result of the subdivision of the day which has been attained by some means or other. The actual measurement of the hours, and possibly their subdivisions, that is, the telling of the time of day, was probably effected by means of hour-glasses, or clepsydras, or sun-dials. A people of so high a cultural and technical standard will certainly have had efficient time-measuring contrivances. Like all other parts of the Calendar,

130

also the 'hour' panels must have been used for counting purposes. What was computed will be elaborated below.

With this I conclude my analysis of the symbolism of the amazing Calendar of Kalasasaya and my review of the labours of Posnansky and Kiss. Though much, no doubt, still remains hidden—an incentive to other, better minds—a wealth of interesting material lies already before us.

Its evaluation has been attempted in the following Section.

The Chronological Evaluation of the Calendar of Kalasasaya

By F. L. Ashton

It has been shown in the foregoing analysis that the great sculptured frieze on the monumental gate of the Temple of Kalasasaya gathers 290 of the 447 symbols figured on its main part into twelve subdivisions, each of which consists of 24 symbols. These symbols are arranged in the form of 'haloes' surrounding impressive heads. The whole design is so striking, and seems so full of meaning, that one feels urged to regard it not as a merely arbitrary feature of the nature of an involved ornament, but rather as a record, obviously of something that, while it is a whole, is also subdivisible, or definitely requires subdivision.

It has been suggested that this meander-embraced array of haloed heads constitutes a Calendar of a year of 290 days, subdivided into twelve 'Twelfths', ten of them comprising 24 days, and two 25 days. As has been mentioned before this interpretation is based on certain remarkable calculations by the Austrian cosmologist, Hans Hoerbiger.

It will be shown in what follows that, in spite of its singularity, this interpretation was essentially correct. Hence, the peculiar lay-out of the Calendar cannot have been the result merely of the ultimately unfathomable whim of an *artist*, but is really deeply senseful, and could not, in fact, be drawn up in any other way. It constitutes the eloquent record, observed by a *scientist*, of actual conditions obtaining at the time when the great chronographic frieze was sculptured.

The reason for this arrangement of the day symbols into twelve groups becomes immediately clear when the apparent movements of the Sun and the former Satellite are analysed. If these bodies moved as predicted by Hoerbiger, there must have resulted a distinct twenty-four day cycle of events. Hence, there seems to be every reason for supposing that it was their observations of this cycle of events that led the astronomers of Tiahuanaco to divide the year into twelve parts. The 'twelfths' of the Tiahanaco year would thus be *natural* subdivisions, in contradistinction to the twelve months of our year, the reason for whose number is quite obscure, and probably arbitrary. The most impressive astronomical events in those days were, without doubt, the eclipses—above all, of course, the solar ones. However, these eclipses of the Sun would be too frequent, and would, moreover, occur too irregularly, to be primarily useful for making chronological divisions. On the other hand, eclipses taking place at some particular time—for instance, at sunrise, noon, or sunset—would occur periodically. As will be shown presently it was, indeed, these special eclipses, and certain other important features of the Satellite's movements which provided the cycle on which the Tiahuanacan 'twelfth' was based.

The first stage in the analysis of the movements of the Satellite, relative to the Sun and to the Earth's surface, is to work out a number of elements. These are given in Table I, wherein everything except the angle subtended by the Satellite's disk[60] follows from the three figures given at the top, namely, the number of days in a year, the number of lunations in a year, and the length, in hours, of a year.

It has been shown in the foregoing that the numbers 290 and 447 appear on the calendar sculpture as the totals of certain groups of symbols. Theoretical considerations allowed us to address the former figure as the number of days in a year at that time, and the latter as the number of the Satellite's

THE CALENDAR OF KALASASAYA

TABLE I

No. of Solar days in year	290
No. of Lunations in year	447
Length of year	8766 hrs.

From which it may be deduced that—

Length of a Solar day	30·2276 hrs.

Let it be supposed, for the sake of simplicity, that—

30·2276 modern hrs. = 30 T/hrs.

Then it may be deduced that—

Length of a Solar day	30 T/hrs.
Length of a year	8700 T/hrs.
Satellite's Lunation period	19·4631 T/hrs.
Satellite's revolution period, relative to the Earth's surface	55·4140 T/hrs.
No. of Lunations in 24 days	36·9931
No. of revolutions of Satellite, relative to earth's surface, in 24 days	12·9931
No. of these revolutions in one year	157
No. of visible solar eclipses in 24 days	19
Earth's angular velocity of rotation, relative to the Sun	12° per T/hr.
Satellite's angular velocity of revolution, relative to the Sun	18° 30′ per T/hr.
Satellite's angular velocity of revolution, relative to the Earth's surface	6° 30′ per T/hr.
Angle subtended by Satellite's disk	6° 48′
Time taken by Satellite to move across its own breadth	1·047 T/hrs.

Discrepancies:

Excess of eclipse cycle over 24 days	0·1342 T/hrs.
Excess of 13 Satellite revolutions, relative to Earth's surface, over 24 days	0·3820 T/hrs.

lunations. As previously stated in this book the length of the year has been accepted as 8766 hours, its present length.

The actual time unit to be employed is unimportant from the point of view of these calculations; what is important is the ratio of the lengths of a day and a lunation. It appears from the symbolism of the thirty winged figures in the lateral panels of the calendar sculpture that the Tiahuanacans subdivided their day into thirty 'hours'. Hence, in order to simplify the calculations, a time equal to one thirtieth of a Tiahuanacan day has been used instead of the modern hour: this has been called a 'Tiahuanaco Hour', or a 'T/hour'.

While the Satellite's actual lunation period, as seen by an extra-terrestrial observer, and as calculable by a terrestrial one, was 19·4631 T/hours, the apparent revolution period of the Satellite, relative to the Earth's surface, was 55·414 T/hours. The Satellite appeared to move so slowly because it had to overtake the rotating Earth. On the other hand, its progress over the background of the fixed stars would have been much more rapid than the apparent movement of the Sun. It must not be forgotten, when considering the argument given below, that at that time the Satellite rose in the west and set in the east.

The Satellite rose, and set, 13 times in each 24 day period, and this figure is recorded on the Calendar by the 13 symbols of the pedestal on which the figure of the First Twelfth stands. In the course of a year it rose and set 157 times, a figure which is also recorded by a group of symbols[61]. Finally, the number 19, being the number of visible solar eclipses in a 24 day period, might be expected to have been recorded. If the symbols on the figure of the First Twelfth are examined it is seen that 19 of them are condor's heads which may be taken to represent the number of solar eclipses[62].

There would be an equal number of satellitic eclipses. Though they would be of no chronographic value they might nevertheless be expected to be referred to on this wonderful piece of sculpture, for the sake of the *completeness* of the record, if for nothing else. Indeed, we find a total of 19 satellitic symbols on the body of the First Twelfth, which number might be interpreted as descriptive of events in which something happened to the Satellite. And if the halo of the First Twelfth is examined it is found to consist only of satellitic symbols, which are, significantly, divided into two groups: 19 + 5. This persistent recurrence of the number 19 seems to be intended as a record stressing the number of either sort of eclipse.

The Twenty-Four Day Cycle

It will be seen from Table I that 37 lunations and 13 apparent revolutions of the Satellite almost exactly coincided with 24 days. This gave rise to a 24 day cycle of events which appears to have been the obvious source of the 24 day period, or Twelfth.

As is only to be expected the actual movements of the Earth and the Satellite, and the notation of these movements on the calendar sculpture, did not exactly agree. Though these discrepancies, or incommensurabilities, were very small they could not be neglected, because they accumulated with time. Sooner or later, measures had to be taken to compensate for them. This will be dealt with later; for the present the 24 day cycle will be discussed.

There were a number of events which would have been useful for chronological purposes. They were:

(a) the eclipse of the Sun at sunrise,
(b) the eclipse of the Sun at sunset,
(c) the eclipse of the Sun at noon,
(d) the rising of the Satellite at sunrise,
(e) the setting of the Satellite at sunset,
(f) the rising of the Satellite at noon,
(g) the setting of the Satellite at noon,
(h) the rising of the Satellite at midnight, and
(i) the setting of the Satellite at midnight.

Each of these events would have occurred periodically, and they would have made up a 24 day cycle.

135

TABLE II

Calendar for One Twelfth

Day		Satellite rises	Satellite sets	Solar Eclipses	Remarks
1.	Day		0·00	0·00	The rising sun is eclipsed
	Night	27·71		19·46	by the setting Satellite.
2.	Day			8·93	
	Night		25·41	28·39	
3.	Day				
	Night	23·12		17·85	
4.	Day			7·32	Eclipse at noon.
	Night		20·83	26·78	
5.	Day				
	Night	18·53		16·24	
6.	Day			5·70	
	Night		16·24	25·17	
7.	Day	13·95		14·63	The setting Sun is eclip-
	Night				sed by the rising Satellite.
8.	Day		11·65	4·09	
	Night			23·56	
9.	Day	9·36		13·02	
	Night				
10,	Day		7·07	2·48	The Satellite sets at noon.
	Night			21·95	
11.	Day	4·77		11·41	
	Night				
12.	Day		2·48	0·87	
	Night			20·33	

Day		Satellite rises	Satellite sets	Solar Eclipses	Remarks
13.	Day	0·19		9·80	The Satellite rises at sun-
	Night		27·89	29·26	rise.
14.	Day				
	Night	25·60		18·72	
15.	Day			8·19	
	Night		23·31	27·65	
16.	Day				The Satellite rises at mid-
	Night	21·01		17·11	night.
17.	Day			6·58	
	Night		18·72	26·04	
18.	Day				
	Night	16·43		15·50	
19.	Day		14·14	4·96	The Satellite sets at sun-
	Night			24·43	set.
20.	Day	11·84		13·89	
	Night				
21.	Day		9·55	3·35	
	Night			22·82	
22.	Day	7·26		12·28	The Satellite rises at noon.
	Night				
23.	Day		4·96	1·74	
	Night			21·21	
24.	Day	2·67		10·67	
	Night				

First day of Second Twelfth

1.	Day		0·38	0·13	The rising Sun is again
	Night	28·08		19·59	eclipsed by the setting
					Satellite.

From the information contained in Table I it is possible to prepare a calendar and include in it the rising and setting times of the Satellite and the times of solar eclipses. Eclipses of the Satellite would not have been of much value, as they would have been long-drawn-out affairs with no clear beginnings and endings; they have therefore not been taken into consideration. The calendar is given in Table II. It will be seen that the Tiahuanaco thirty-hour-day has been reckoned as having started at sunrise; it makes no difference to our argument whether the Tiahuanacans actually did so, or not. Thus, *at the Equinoxes*, the four main times of the day would have occurred as follows:

$$
\begin{aligned}
\text{Sunrise} &= 00 \cdot 00 \text{ T/hours,} \\
\text{Noon} &= 07 \cdot 50 \text{ T/hours,} \\
\text{Sunset} &= 15 \cdot 00 \text{ T/hours, and} \\
\text{Midnight} &= 22 \cdot 50 \text{ T/hours.}
\end{aligned}
$$

Here, as everywhere, fractions of a T/hour have been expressed as decimals.

It will be seen from Table II that not only did all the events listed above, with the exception of (i), occur, but they also *occurred at regular intervals, with two blank days between each.* If we now examine any of the haloes[63] we find that the sculptor has arranged his symbols in strict accordance with this cycle of events: he has marked these 'special' days by 'special' symbols: the heads of plumed pumas, condors, toxodons, or elongated disks. The two 'blank' days, however, he has pictured by what we may, to all intents and purposes, interpret here as—blanks.

The various events did not, of course, occur exactly at their theoretically correct times—they could hardly be expected to have done so—but it must not be forgotten that the Satellite took over an hour to rise, or set, and that solar eclipses would have often lasted for up to about a third of that time: $0 \cdot 34$ T/hours. A certain margin might therefore have been allowed on either side, which would have covered all the discrepancies, except for that on the 16th day. In strict accordance with the

138

cycle of events the Satellite was to have *risen* at midnight on this day: however, it was actually already clear of the horizon an hour before midnight; but, moving as slowly as it did its altitude was only about 6°. This day, therefore, was the one 'weak spot' in the whole scheme, but that is no argument against it. The events on all the other 'special days' occurring in strict accordance with the theory, the original calendar makers, anxious to make their scheme symmetrical, may well be conceived as having decided to ignore the slight flaw, seeing that, firstly, it was so near an approximation, and, secondly, after all an event of minor importance.

Each Twelfth was naturally divided into four sections. During the first, which was inaugurated by the eclipse of the Sun at sunrise, the Satellite rose and set only during the hours of darkness. During the second, inaugurated by the eclipse of the Sun at sunset, the Satellite rose and set during daylight hours. The third section was inaugurated by the Satellite rising at sunrise, and during it the Satellite rose and set at night. In the fourth, inaugurated by the Satellite setting at sunset, the Satellite rose and set during the day.

The symmetry of the cycle of events can best be shown by setting the calendar out in circular form. This has been done in Diagram 21 and it will probably be agreed that this is the clearest way of doing it. This will become still more apparent when the question of the compensation for discrepancies is discussed. It will be appreciated that we have thus been able to reveal the reason why the design whereby each Twelfth is represented in circular form was adopted.

In view of the division of the Twelfth into four sections there can be little doubt that the 0°, 90°, 180°, and 270° positions were filled by the 'principal' events, (a), (b), (d), and (e); but there may be some doubt as to which of these four 'principal' events was taken as the beginning of the Twelfth. There are, however, weighty reasons for believing that the first day of each Twelfth was reckoned when event(a) occurred: that is, when the rising Sun was eclipsed by the setting

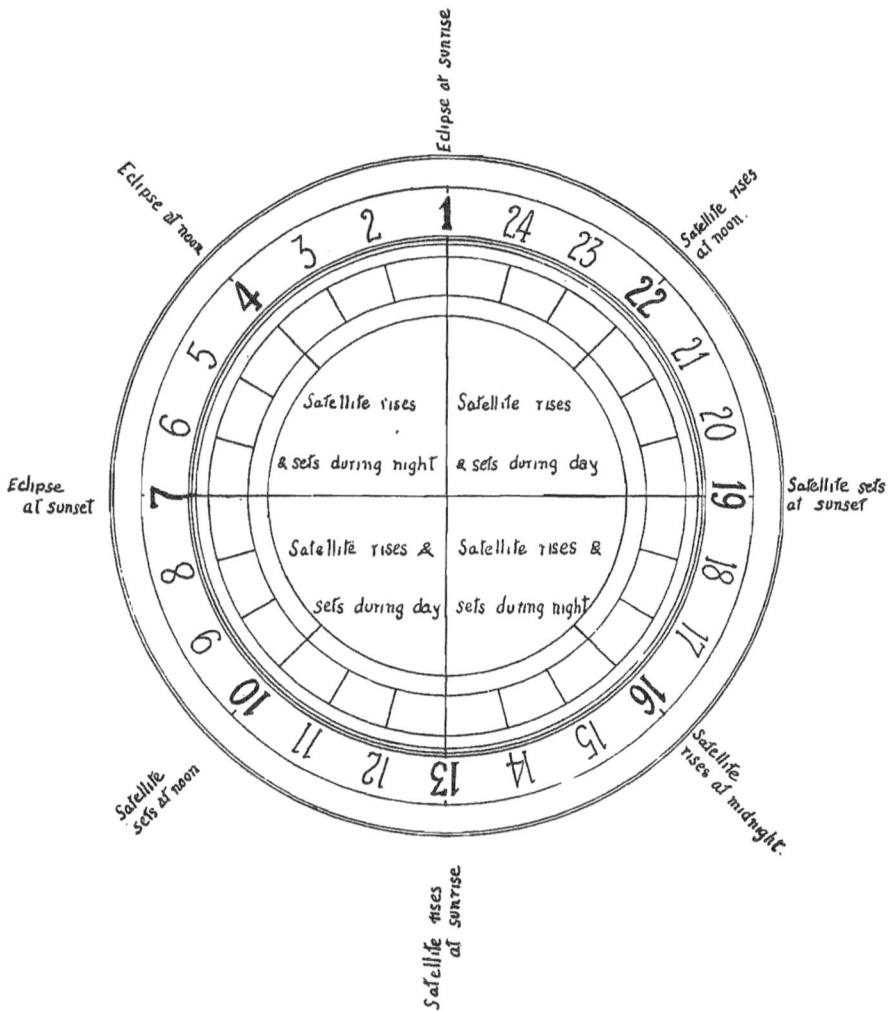

Eclipse at sunrise

Eclipse at noon

Satellite rises at noon

Eclipse at sunset

Satellite sets at sunset

Eclipse at sunset

Satellite rises & sets during night | Satellite rises & sets during day

Satellite rises & sets during day | Satellite rises & sets during night

Satellite sets at noon

Satellite rises at midnight

Satellite rises at sunrise

DIAGRAM 21

Scheme of the Twelfths of the Tiahuanaco Calendar

140

Satellite. This supposition would indeed be well supported by the significant form of the symbol used to designate the first day of each Twelfth.

The first day of the year was most probably fixed by the conjunction of the Sun with a certain group of stars. The makers of the Calendar had the great advantage over astronomers of subsequent ages in that they could readily observe the stars shining round the Sun during its frequent eclipses, and leisurely and deliberately, too, because of their considerable length. It would be natural then to begin the new year with a solar eclipse. Two of the four principal events of each Twelfth were eclipses—the eclipse at sunrise and the eclipse at sunset. Of the two the eclipse at sunrise seems to be the more probable, for a dawn phenomenon is the more likely one to be accepted as the beginning of a period. However, it would make no difference to the main argument here developed, which was adopted.

The first dawn of each Twelfth must have been an impressive sight. During the preceding night the huge Satellite has shone brightly, moving slowly towards the east and waning steadily as it goes. As it nears the horizon it shrinks to a narrow crescent which pales, and then vanishes, in the rapidly growing brilliance of a tropical dawn. When no trace of the Satellite can be seen any more, and when the Sun seems to be on the very point of rising—the light fades with bewildering suddenness, darkness more intense than that of the preceding night descends, and the stars blaze forth again. And now on the eastern horizon the vast dark disk of the Satellite can be seen, mantled by the Sun's corona which grows steadily brighter directly above it until the disk seems to be crowned with a magnificent plume, or crest. Then, at last, the Sun appears above the Satellite's limb, daylight floods back, and, in no more than a minute, not a trace of the Satellite can be seen, for it has sunk away out of sight, below the horizon. The Sun, however, rises gloriously, and shines with unchallenged splendour throughout the following day.

Such an impressive spectacle, deeply symbolic of the victory

141

of the Sun over the Satellite, might well have been taken to inaugurate the new year, and indeed each of the Twelfths throughout the year.

Let us now compare the halo symbols with the events which they represented:

Day	Event	Description	Symbol
1.	(a)	Eclipse of the Sun at sunrise	
13.	(d)	Satellite rises at sunrise	
7.	(b)	Eclipse of the Sun at *sunset*	
19.	(e)	Satellite sets at *sunset*	
4.	(c)	Eclipse of the Sun at *noon*	
10.	(g)	Satellite sets at *noon*	
22.	(f)	Satellite rises at *noon*	
16.	(h)	Satellite rises at midnight	

The days without 'key-events'—2, 3, 5, 6, 8, 9, 11, 12, 14, 15, 17, 18, 20, 21, 23, 24—were expressed by disks:

It appears that for some reason the condor's head was used to characterize events that took place at sunset, and the toxodon's head those that took place at noon. An exception to this rule was again on the 16th day, which has already been described as constituting the one flaw in the scheme, but this one discrepancy was not allowed to interfere with the symmetry of

142

the design. The satellite was 'full' at noon on this day, and there was a symmetry about the earth-satellite-sun system which was equalled only by that of the 4th day when the satellite was 'new' at noon. There was, therefore, a definite 'noon event' on the 16th day which may not have escaped the Tiahuanacan astronomers.

It will be seen from Table II that the 13th day was the only day in the Twelfth on which the Satellite both rose and set in the course of one day. The day was, in a sense, 'spanned' by the Satellite, since rising at dawn it shone throughout the day and for most of the night. That is obviously the reason why the disk, the satellitic symbol *par excellence*, is used in a special 'elongated' form at the 13th position. This surmise is supported by a symbolism in the figure of the First Twelfth where the elongated disk appears 'spanned' by a 'puma-headed fish',[64] a personification of the Satellite.

Finally, the 'plumed puma', set so dominatingly at the top of each head, evidently characterized the dark disk of the Satellite resting upon the eastern horizon, with the rays of the Sun's corona rising vertically above it.

Many interesting features of the 24 day cycle are brought out when altitude-time curves are drawn for the sun and satellite. This has been done in Diagram 22, in which the altitudes are plotted against time in T/hrs. throughout one Twelfth, night-time being shown by shaded areas. The 13 passages of the satellite across the sky are numbered with Roman numerals, and it can be seen at a glance how much of each passage was made by day and how much by night. All the eclipses of the sun are shown, those above and on the zero line being visible at Tiahuanaco and those below it being invisible from there.

The natural divisions of the Twelfth, caused by astronomical events, can now be seen more clearly. For example:

During the first and third sections:

1. There were three eclipses of the Sun (on alternate days);
2. On alternate days the sky was free from the Satellite; and
3. The Satellite was visible for some portion of every night.

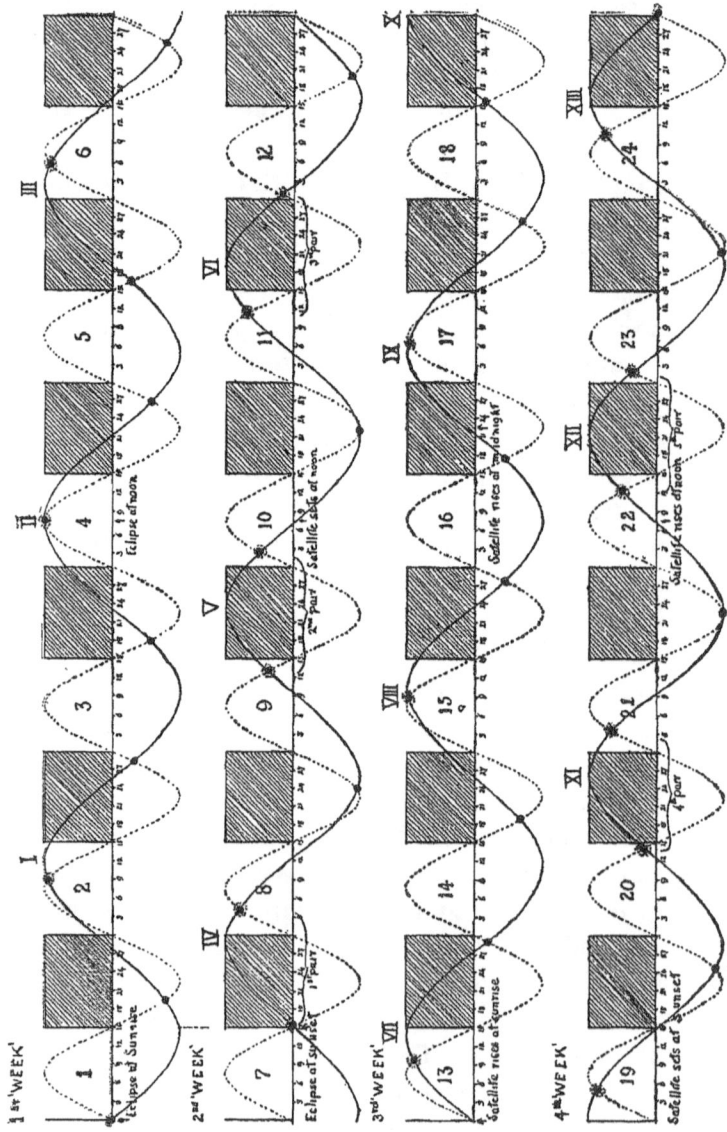

DIAGRAM 22

Altitudes of the Sun (...) and of the Satellite (—) plotted against time in T/hrs. Solar eclipses are indicated by dots at intersections of the two curves.

During the second and fourth sections:

1. There were six eclipses of the Sun (one each day);
2. The Satellite was visible for some portion of every day; and
3. On alternate nights the sky was free from the Satellite.

The thirteen symbols on the pedestal of the figure of the First Twelfth (Diagram 19) have already been identified with the thirteen passages of the Satellite across the sky in 24 days. Six of these symbols are the heads of condors, six are the heads of pumas, two of which are crowned, and one is the puma-headed 'fish'. With the aid of Diagram 22 these can now be tentatively assigned to the various passages of the Satellite across the sky, as follows:

Type of Passage	Passage No.	Symbol
	I	
Satellite rises, waxing, at	II	
night, eclipses Sun on the	III	
following day, and sets,	VIII	Condors' heads
waning, during following	IX	
night	(X)	
Satellite rises, waning, by		
day, eclipses Sun, shines	V	
throughout night, eclipses	VI	
Sun on the following morn-	XI	Pumas' heads
ing, and sets, waxing, during	XII	
day		
Satellite eclipses Sun while		
rising, shines throughout	IV	Crowned puma's head
night, and sets, waxing, dur-		
ing following day		
Satellite rises, waning, by		
day and eclipses Sun. It		
shines throughout the follow-	XIII	Crowned puma's head
ing night and eclipses Sun at		
sunrise while setting		

Type of Passage	Passage No.	Symbol
Satellite rises at sunrise, full, and sets during following night (i.e. it rises and sets on the same day)	VII	Puma-headed fish[65]

It may be objected that a special symbol should have been provided by the sculptor for passage X. If, however, we take it that in this one instance reference was made to the condition of the Satellite when rising, this would not have been necessary.

Diagram 22 reveals also another matter of interest. It will be seen that, on some occasions, the Satellite twice eclipsed the Sun during a single crossing of the sky. (Cf. Note 62). These paired eclipses occurred during passages IV, V, VI, XI, XII, and XIII, but this last pair was split because its second eclipse took place in the following Twelfth. There were therefore five pairs of eclipses in one Twelfth. The condors' heads on the body of the figure of the First Twelfth have already been identified with eclipses of the Sun. If these are examined it will be seen that those clustering together on the breast of the figure are paired, and each pair firmly tied with a 'double knot' (Non-Numerical Symbol 2), and that there are five pairs in all. (Cf. Diagram 19.)

Compensating for the Discrepancy

We have seen from Table I that 37 lunations did not exactly coincide with 24 days. If the Satellite had revolved only very slightly faster round the Earth than it did, taking 19·4595 T/hours for one lunation instead of 19·4631 T/hours, there would have been no discrepancy at all. Because the discrepancy is so small it was necessary, in this analysis, to retain so many decimal places. Some such discrepancy is, of course, only to be expected, and a calendar that shows evidence of measures taken to compensate for one is more likely to be a genuine article, constructed for practical purposes, than one that does not.

According to the calendar sculpture the Tiahuanacan year

146

contained 290 days, which is not a multiple of 24; consequently extra days had to be added to two of the Twelfths. It will now be shown how these two extra days could have been used to compensate for the small discrepancy mentioned above.

If Table II is examined it will be seen what happened as the discrepancy accumulated with the passage of time. On the first day of the Second Twelfth the eclipse took place at 0·13 T/hours, instead of at 0·00 T/hours, on the first day of the Third Twelfth it took place at 0·26 T/hours, and so on. As the Twelfths went by the eclipse would have taken place later and later, until it could no longer be called a dawn eclipse any more. Therefore some sort of an adjustment had to be made.

It will be seen that on the thirteenth day there was an eclipse at 29·26 T/hours, that is, about three quarters of a T/hour before sunrise. It is clear that not many Twelfths would have had to go by before there was a dawn eclipse at the beginning of the *fourteenth* day. In other words: conditions that had obtained on the first day now occurred on the fourteenth; similarly, conditions that had obtained on the 4th, 7th, 10th, 13th, 16th, 19th, and 22nd occurred on the 17th, 20th, 23rd, 2nd, 5th, 8th, and 11th, respectively. In fact, as can be gathered with the aid of Diagram 21 there was a change-over from each day to the day following the one diametrically opposite it. As the precision of what we may call the First Cycle of Events grew less, the precision of a Second Cycle, identical in all respects, but beginning on the fourteenth day of the Twelfth, grew greater. In order to compensate for this discrepancy the First Cycle had to be abandoned and the Second Cycle adopted. Two things had to be done to make this change-over:

First—An extra day had to be added, at the beginning of the Sixth Twelfth. This had the effect of giving the halo-symbols whose scheme is shown in Diagram 21 a twist through 15°, so that the 'new' thirteenth day coincided with the 'old' fourteenth day;

Secondly—The halo-symbols in that Twelfth had to be read

147

from the bottom instead of from the top, so that the Twelfth actually began with the day characterized by the elongated disk.

Some such ruling as the following one may have been laid down by the makers of the Calendar:

'At the beginning of the Sixth Twelfth, the Sun will be seen to rise fully above the horizon before it is eclipsed. That day will, therefore, not be counted as the first day of the new Twelfth but as an extra day. The day following will be of the elongated disk type, and on it the Satellite will rise at sunrise. This day will be deemed to be the true beginning of the Twelfth and the dawn eclipse will not occur until the 14th day. The Seventh and Eighth Twelfths will also begin with days on which the Satellite rises at sunrise. Another extra day will be added *at the end of the Eighth Twelfth* and the Twelfths there-after will begin again in the normal way, with dawn eclipses.'

This presupposed ruling should cause no head-shaking—for it is not proposed by us, but is actually contained in the symbolism of the Sixth Twelfth. A fish, a satellitic symbol, comes 'flown' on, that is, is to be added. It is attached to the *left* side of the halo, and therefore swims against its anti-clockwise movement; obviously it is supposed to go as far as it can, that is, to the position after the miscarried beginning of the Twelfth. This new second day is to be of the 'elongated disk type', on which the Satellite rises at sunrise, the 'pointer' being the oval symbol contained within the flying fish. The vertical position of the fish wishes to show that something is to be 'transferred' from top to bottom, that is, to its diametrically opposite place. This 'something' is evidently the event which is featured by the corona-sheaf, and which has not yet come off: and this is actually pictured by the 'plume-like tail' of the fish, a reference to the dawn eclipse as clear as it can be desired.

However, before not so very long this arrangement would have had to be abandoned, and another change-over made. From Table II it will be seen that in the First Twelfth of the year an eclipse occurred 1·61 T/hours before the sunrise of the third day. Now, the excess of the eclipse cycle over 24 days,

0·1342 T/hours, multiplied by 12 gives 1·61, so that by the end of the year this difference would have vanished, and this would have been the eclipse which heralded the new year. The change-over to this new cycle, the Third Cycle, was naturally made as soon as necessary. The second of the two supernumerary days was added, at the end of the Eighth Twelfth. And the next twelfth, the Ninth Twelfth, began again with the regular dawn eclipse day.

Effect of the Southern Latitude of Tiahuanaco

At first sight it might appear that the first change-over was belated and that the second was premature. If Tiahuanaco had been situated on the Equator this would have been the case, but, as will now be shown, it was the effect of its southern latitude upon the times of the Sun's rising that caused the designers of the Calendar of Kalasasaya to add their extra days where they did. There are, in fact, no other places in the Calendar where they might have been added and have given the same precision.

In Table III the approximate times of sunrise[66] are given, in the first sub-columns of each of the five main columns, for the first and thirteenth days of each Twelfth as observed from the five latitudes entered at the heads of the main columns. The assumption has been made that the year began with the autumnal equinox[67], (i.e. when the Sun crossed the celestial Equator from S. to N.). The reason for this will become evident as the present argument is developed. The equinoxes and solstices must have taken place round about the first days of the First and Seventh, and of the Fourth and Tenth, Twelfths, respectively, though there was probably no great precision about these.[68]

For the purpose of this analysis the day of 30 T/hours is supposed to have officially begun 7·5 T/hours before noon, i.e. the crossing of the meridian by the Sun. Minus signs indicate that the Sun rose before the 'official' beginning of the day. For

149

example: for the first day of the Tenth Twelfth in latitude 10° S., the sunrise time is recorded as − 0·35 T/hours. This means that it rose 7·85 T/hours before noon, or at 29·65 'o'clock' Tiahuanaco Time on the previous day.

The times, throughout the year, at which the 'dawn' eclipses of the three cycles, discussed above, took place are recorded in the second, third, and fourth sub-columns of the first main column in Table III. The minus signs show when they took place before sunrise. As the sunrise times coincided with the 'official' beginning of the day throughout the year, these figures also give the interval in T/hours, or fractions of a T/hour, that elapsed between the various dawn eclipses and sunrise and are referred to below as the 'discrepancies'. The lowest discrepancy for each Twelfth is recorded in bold type. It may be assumed that in any one Twelfth the cycle that gave the lowest discrepancy would have been the one that would have been used, and that the change-overs from one cycle to the next would have been made accordingly.

The Table makes it quite clear that, at the Equator, the extra days to bring about these change-overs would have had to be added at the beginning of the Fourth Twelfth and at the end of the Ninth.

At 5° S. latitude, however, the sun rose later and later each morning until the winter solstice and, during the winter, the 'Twelfthly' retardation of the dawn eclipses of the first cycle were partially compensated for by this retardation of the Sun's rising. The discrepancies for the first cycle were therefore reduced during the first six Twelfths, as will be seen when the figures in the second sub-column of the 5° main column are compared with those in the second sub-column of that for the Equator. In the same way during the summer Twelfths the sun rose earlier and thereby reduced the discrepancies between sunrise and the dawn eclipses of the third cycle, all of which took place before the 'official' beginning of the day. Another effect of the change of latitude was to delay the change-over from the first cycle to the second until the beginning of the

150

TABLE III

Latitude Twelfth	Day	Equator Sun-rise	Eq. Cycle 1	Eq. Cycle 2	Eq. Cycle 3	5° Sun-rise	5° Cycle 1	5° Cycle 2	5° Cycle 3	10° Sun-rise	10° Cycle 1	10° Cycle 2	10° Cycle 3	15° Sun-rise	15° Cycle 1	15° Cycle 2	15° Cycle 3	20° Sun-rise	20° Cycle 1	20° Cycle 2	20° Cycle 3	25° Sun-rise	25° Cycle 1	25° Cycle 2	25° Cycle 3
1	1	0·00	0·00			0·00	0·00			0·00	0·00			0·00	0·00			0·00	0·00			0·00	0·00		
1	15	0·00		—0·74	—1·61	0·04		—0·78	—1·61	0·13		—0·85	—1·61	0·18		—0·84	—1·61	0·25		—0·92	—1·61	0·23		—0·97	—1·61
2	1	0·00	0·13			0·09	0·04			0·26	0·05			0·36	0·07			0·46	0·08			0·46	0·21		
2	15	0·00		—0·61	—1·48	0·12		—0·73	—1·57	0·37		—0·83	—1·65	0·50		—0·87	—1·74	0·64		—0·87	—1·84	0·64		—0·84	—1·94
3	1	0·00	0·27			0·15	0·12			0·46	0·23			0·61	0·23			0·79	0·31			0·79	0·51		
3	15	0·00		—0·47	—1·54	0·16		—0·65	—1·48	0·50		—0·80	—1·64	0·68		—0·80	—1·80	0·79		—0·79	—1·95	0·87		—0·79	—2·13
4	1	0·00	0·40			0·17	0·23			0·52	0·50			0·71	0·41			0·91	0·51			0·91	0·80		
4	15	0·00		—0·34	—1·21	0·16		—0·50	—1·38	0·50		—0·67	—1·56	0·68		—0·75	—1·75	0·79		—0·79	—1·92	0·87		—0·82	—2·12
5	1	0·00	0·55			0·15	0·38			0·46	0·80			0·61	0·80			0·61	1·30			0·79	1·40		
5	15	0·00		—0·20	—1·07	0·12		—0·38	—1·22	0·37		—0·44	—1·37	0·50		—0·57	—1·55	0·64		—0·70	—1·50	0·64		—0·30	—1·40
6	1	0·00	0·67			0·09	0·58			0·26	1·11			0·36	1·20			0·50	1·67			0·46	1·86		
6	15	0·00		—0·07	—0·94	0·04		—0·32	—1·05	0·13		—0·16	—1·11	0·18		—0·20	—1·20	0·25		—0·25	—1·02	0·23		0·28	—0·80
7	1	0·00	0·80			0·00	0·80			0·09	1·37			0·00	1·55			0·00	1·92			0·00	2·12		
7	15	0·00		0·05	—0·80	—0·04		—0·11	—0·80	0·00		0·16	—0·80	—0·13		0·55	—0·80	—0·18		0·68	—0·80	—0·23		0·82	—0·30
8	1	0·00	0·94			—0·09	1·05			—0·13	1·56			—0·26	1·75			—0·36	1·95			—0·46	2·15		
8	15	0·00		0·18	—0·67	—0·12		0·09	—0·58	—0·26		0·42	—0·50	—0·37		0·81	—0·41	—0·46		0·99	—0·31	—0·64		1·18	—0·21
9	1	0·00	1·07			—0·15	1·25			—0·46	1·57			—0·46	1·73			—0·64	1·95			—0·79	1·94		
9	15	0·00		0·31	—0·53	—0·16		0·30	—0·28	—0·50		0·64	—0·23	—0·50		0·95	—0·07	—0·79		1·02	—0·08	—0·87		1·32	0·13
10	1	0·00	1·21			—0·17	1·38			—0·52	1·58			—0·50	1·80			—0·87	1·84			—0·91	2·15		
10	15	0·00		0·45	—0·40	—0·16		0·47	—0·23	—0·50		0·78	—0·05	—0·57		0·95	0·12	—0·91		1·08	0·25	—0·87		1·52	0·33
11	1	0·00	1·34			—0·15	1·49			—0·50	1·64			—0·50	1·74			—0·87	1·92			—0·79	1·94		
11	15	0·00		0·58	—0·27	—0·12		0·61	—0·12	—0·46		0·82	—0·04	—0·62		0·95	0·19	—0·79		1·15	0·36	—0·64		1·22	0·52
12	1	0·00	1·48			—0·09	1·57			—0·37	1·65			—0·26	1·67			—0·64	1·95			—0·46	1·18		
12	15	0·00		0·71	—0·13	—0·04		0·70	—0·04	—0·13		0·82	—0·03	—0·50		0·95	0·13	—0·50		1·08	0·23	—0·25		1·94	0·26
Mean discrepancy		0·20				0·16				0·12				0·15				0·23				0·35			

THE CALENDAR OF KALASASAYA

Fifth Twelfth and to bring forward the change-over to the third cycle to the end of the Eighth Twelfth. There was also a reduction in the mean discrepancy, showing that this small change in latitude increased the efficiency of the system.

At 10° S. latitude the retardation of the sunrise began to over-compensate for the retardation of the dawn eclipses of the first cycle, so that these eclipses of the Second and Third Twelfths actually took place before sunrise. The discrepancies were however small, no more than a couple of minutes or so. Similar over-compensations occurred, with the third cycle, during the Eleventh and Twelfth Twelfths. The change-over from the first to the second cycle was retarded and must have taken place at the beginning of the Sixth Twelfth, though the change-over from the second to the third remained at the end of the Eighth. There was a further reduction in the mean discrepancy to 0·12 T/hours, or round about 7 minutes.

At 15° S. latitude the over-compensations became sufficiently great to reduce the efficiency of the system, and the change-over from the second to the third cycle was brought forward to the end of the Seventh Twelfth. Farther south than 20° the seasonal variations in the times of sunrise made the scheme very inefficient and, moreover, the second cycle became largely unnecessary.

The results of the analysis contained in Table III may be summarised as follows:

Latitude	0°	5°	10°	15°	20°	25°
Mean Discrepancy.	0·20	0·16	0·12	0·15	0·23	0·33
Twelfth at the beginning of which the first change-over had to be made.	4th.	5th.	6th.	6th.	7th.	7th.
Twelfth at the end of which the second change-over had to be made.	9th.	8th.	8th.	7th.	7th.	7th.

These figures can leave little doubt that, if the argument developed here is correct, *the Calendar of Kalasasaya was designed for the use of people living in latitude 10° S.*

151

The present latitude of Tiahuanaco is $16\frac{1}{2}°$ S., but there are certain reasons for supposing that the position of the Poles, and consequently of the Equator, have changed slightly since the end of the Tertiary Era, and moreover that Tiahuanaco was nearer to the Equator in those days than it is today.[69] In fact its latitude might very well have been in the neighbourhood of 10° S. That it is possible to link the positions of the two 'flying fish' Twelfths with the latitude of Tiahuanaco is remarkable and offers a powerful corroboration of the theory.

Other Discrepancies

It is, of course, highly improbable that 447 lunations and 290 days exactly coincided with each other and with the length of the year. There would therefore have been two other discrepancies to tax the ingenuity of the designers of the Calendar.

The first of these, which arose because 447 lunations did not exactly equal 290 days, was probably very small. But however small it was it would have accumulated with the passing years, and sooner or later an adjustment would have had to be made for it. This could have been done by either adding a day to, or dropping a day from, one of the Twelfths when it became necessary.

The second discrepancy would have been more difficult to deal with. It cannot be supposed that the dawn eclipse at the beginning of the 'thirteenth' Twelfth occurred exactly at the autumnal equinox year after year. Such coincidences simply do not happen. That there was a discrepancy between the 290 day cycle and the true length of the year can be taken for granted, the only questions are—how large was it? and—how could it be compensated for?

There are, however, grounds for believing that it was not very large. We have analysed in some detail the phenomena resulting from a year of 290 days and 447 lunations of the Satellite, and we have endeavoured to show that these could have very well formed the basis of the calendar system of

152

Kalasasaya. These phenomena must have been presented to the observers in no uncertain manner for many years or the system would never have been adopted at all. In fact we may assume that the 290 day cycle must have coincided very closely with the year, for if different numbers of days and lunations had been involved then phenomena which would have led to the adoption of a different scheme would have been observed.

Nevertheless, even if the discrepancy was very small, a matter of minutes only, it would have accumulated with the passing years and sooner or later have made itself felt. In dealing with it, the Tiahuanacans would have been faced with the same problem that has always arisen when men have tried to reconcile the lunar month with the solar year. The discrepancy between the twelve lunar months and one year is so large that most peoples have sooner or later abandoned the attempt and either gone, like Julius Caesar, wholly by the Sun, or, like Mohammed, wholly by the Moon. The only people who appear to have been successful in combining the two were the Babylonians. Their method was to intercalate, every so often, whole months into a year which normally contained exactly twelve lunar months. This is the method that would have had to be used also at Tiahuanaco.

As the years went by, and the dawn eclipse heralding the new year strayed further and further from the equinox, there would have been only one way in which it could be brought back again. The discrepancies would have had to be allowed to accumulate until they amounted to twelve days and then a whole Twelfth would have had to have been added to, or dropped from, the year. This would have had the effect of either advancing or retarding the equinox, in relation to the inaugurating eclipse, by the same amount as it had previously lagged behind or been ahead of it. It is possible, however, that the need for this drastic correction never arose, for it appears that 'very soon' after the establishment of the Calendar, Tiahuanaco was lost.

The Thirty Winged Figures

There are two panels of fifteen winged figures each on either side of the figure of the First Twelfth and its pedestal, and the suggestion has been made by Kiss that these represent subdivisions of the day. If this was so then the Tiahuanacan day must, indeed, have contained thirty subdivisions of the same length as the T/hours used in this disquisition. Kiss's guess is supported by the fact that the Satellite took just about one of these to rise and set; and it is possible that the Tiahuanacans, noticing that this period was almost exactly a thirtieth of their day, adopted it as a unit of time.

Kiss does not suggest any use to which these thirty hour-figures may have been put. It is extremely unlikely that they were only featured on the Calendar by the Tiahuanacans to show how they subdivided the day. Everybody must have known that. The panels clearly could not have been used for telling the hour of the day; for this purpose other time-measuring devices must have been employed. However, as the whole Calendar is a counting calendar, these figures also must have been used for counting out something. The most likely surmise, then, is that these figures were designed to be used as a counting-board by which the approximate times of coming eclipses could be calculated. It must not be forgotten that, although eclipses of the Sun occurred at regular intervals, half of them would have been below the horizon and the visible ones would have been anything but regular in occurrence. Sometimes there would be one every day, at other times they would happen every other day. If an eclipse occurred before noon on one day it would probably occur after noon on the next. To flat Earth astronomers, assuming the Tiahuanacans to have been such, there would seem to have been little rhyme or reason about them.

There are certain inconveniences attached to being suddenly plunged into complete darkness, for a time of up to about one third of an hour, when in the midst of one's daily work. On clear days ample warning would have been given because the Satellite would have been seen approaching the Sun; but when the sky was overcast it would have been a different matter: the world would then have been plunged into intense darkness with no warning at all. Men engaged in dangerous pursuits, such as hunting wild animals, navigating dangerous coast-lines, making their ways over difficult mountain sides, would not only have been inconvenienced, but set in peril of their lives. There can be no doubt that it was a matter of great importance to such men to know when the next eclipse was to be expected.

The method of finding this from the winged figures was quite simple. The numbers given below represent the figures, it having been assumed that the first figure on the left represented the first hour of the day. There are, of course, other ways of numbering them; all that is required for the present purpose is that numbers 1 to 15 should be on one side, and numbers 16 to 30 on the other.[70]

Day Side						Night Side				
5	4	3	2	1		16	17	18	19	20
10	9	8	7	6		21	22	23	24	25
15	14	13	12	11		26	27	28	29	30

The rule for finding when the next eclipse was to be expected would be as follows:

'Starting from the figure after the one representing the hour during which the last eclipse took place, count twenty figures. If the twentieth figure lies in the left-hand panel, then an eclipse will take place at that hour on the following day. If, on the other hand, the twentieth figure is to be found in the right-hand panel, then a second twenty figures must be counted, and, if the figure then arrived at lies in the left-hand panel, then there will be an eclipse at that hour on the following day. If, however, in counting this second twenty all the figures of the left-hand panel are passed, then there will be no eclipse on the following day, and a third twenty must be counted.

155

This third twenty is, of course, bound to end in the left-hand panel, and will give the approximate time of the eclipse on the second day.'

As an example of the third case the second day on Table II should be considered. It will be seen that an eclipse took place during the eighth T/hour. Twenty figures must therefore be counted, starting with the ninth figure. The 28th figure is reached, and as this is in the right-hand panel, a second twenty has to be counted. As this second twenty is counted the whole of the left-hand panel will be passed over; and so it may be predicted that there will be no eclipse on the third day. Figure 18 is reached, and a third twenty is counted; this twenty ends with figure 8, which is a close enough approximation to the time of the eclipse on the fourth day of the Twelfth.

If the above theory is correct the number 'twenty' should be given somewhere in the design. It seems to be supplied by the fact that twenty of the winged figures are anthropoid.[71]

It may be thought that the people who designed so ingenious a Calendar could not have needed such an aid for making a simple calculation. But it must not be forgotten that it is our heritage of a wonderful system of notation that makes calculating easy for us. Without it the simplest sum taxes the highest intelligence, and in all probability the men who built such marvels as the pyramids had to resort to the abacus when they made their calculations. The Tiahuanacans had neither our notation, nor our Copernican system of astronomy to aid them. They did not realise that eclipses took place also when the Sun was beneath their horizon. Some such counting board as this would therefore have been essential to them.

It is possible that this was only one of the uses for which the winged figures were designed. There are 22 symbols attached to each of them, which seem to be full of meaning. It seems very likely that they are supposed to be subdivisions of the

T/hours. Maybe further study and analysis will reveal the use they were intended for.

Conclusion

The Calendar of Kalasasaya was designed for a year of 290 days and there can be no doubt that the year it represents was a solar year.

At the time when the Calendar was designed, the year, according to Hoerbiger's followers, actually contained only 290 days. The Earth's rotation was subsequently speeded up by the tidal action of a Satellite which was approaching it at the time and which, a few thousand years later, came so close that it was destroyed by the Earth's gravity.

Various features of the Calendar support this theory, and it may be helpful to summarize these together with the deductions that they support.

1. The total number of symbols on the Calendar is 447.

1. It can be deduced that, when the Earth had 290 days in the year, the Satellite revolved round it about 447 times in that period. It is, of course, impossible to calculate the exact number of revolutions without knowing the mass of the Satellite. Nevertheless Hoerbiger, who knew nothing of the Calendar, gave an estimate which came within $2\frac{1}{2}$ per cent of this.

2. Twelve heads are depicted on the Calendar, indicating this number of subdivisions of the year, and these must, therefore, have contained 24 days each.

2. If 447 lunations of the Satellite are assumed, it can be shown that there would have been a 24 day cycle of conjunctions, quadratures, and oppositions, of the Satellite with the Sun, when it was in special positions relative to the horizon, i.e. rising, setting, or culminating.

157

3. The days are shown in 'haloes' round the heads, i.e. theTwelfths are recorded in circular form.

3. The clearest way of recording the cycle is to set it down in circular form.

4. Every third day is represented by a special symbol.

4. A conjunction, opposition, or quadrature, of the Satellite with the Sun in one of the special positions would occur every third day.

5. Two of the Twelfths have symbols attached to them indicating the addition of an extra day.

5. The cycle would be slightly longer than 24 days, but this discrepancy could be exactly compensated for by twice adding an extra day to a Twelfth in the course of a year.

6. The extra days were added to the Sixth and Eighth Twelfths.

6. It can be shown that for a place situated at the (then) latitude of Tiahuanaco the most efficient method of making the compensation would have been to add the extra days to just these Twelfths.

7. There are 38 symbols on the body of the figure representing the First Twelfth, one of which is a flying fish.

7. There would be 37 lunations in every 24-day Twelfth, and 38 in the 'augmented' Sixth and Eighth Twelfths, denoted by the addition of a flying fish.

8. There are 13 symbols in the pedestal below the figure.

8. The Satellite would make 13 apparent revolutions of the heavens in 24 days.

9. Nineteen of the symbols on the body of the figure of the First Twelfth have condors' heads.

9. There would be nineteen visible conjunctions of the Satellite with the Sun in 24 days. Owing to the large angle subtended by the Satellite most, if not all, of these conjunctions were eclipses.

158

10. Some of the symbols are paired, the number of pairs being five.

10. On five occasions during each Twelfth the Satellite twice eclipsed the Sun during a single crossing of the sky.

11. There are thirty winged figures, arranged in two panels of fifteen.

11. It can be shown that these could have been used as a counting-board, from which the times of future eclipses could be calculated.

F. L. ASHTON

Final Remarks about the Calendar Gate

Thus the thought-tool of Hans Hoerbiger's Cosmological Theory, as wielded by Kiss and myself, and its special, brilliant application by Ashton, allow us to decipher successfully the chronographic system of the remote Tiahuanacans. All other approaches tried hitherto have led nowhere,[72] nor does there seem to be a probability that any new endeavours will lead anywhere. This should count as a point in favour of our Theory.

The chief objection that might be raised against our interpretation of the Calendar is: If we are right, and the sculpture on the monolithic gate of the Sun Temple of Tiahuanaco indeed shows the Calendar of a certain part of an Aeon of our Earth which was, to all intents and purposes, contemporaneous with the last stage of the Tertiary Age, then this piece of sculpture must be exceedingly old, even several hundred thousand years, perhaps. This, it is said, is impossible, for the action of the weather would long have effaced entirely the rather delicate carving, which is remarkably clear-cut.

In answer to this it may be said: The Calendar Gate of Tiahuanaco is made of andesite, a material of almost glassy hardness, which is eminently able to resist the ravages of the weather. Though Tiahuanaco is situated some 12,000 feet above sea-level it is rarely subjected to frosts; besides, the thin air contains only very little carbon dioxide, and no other corrosive gases; the air contains little humidity since practically all

159

moisture is rained off in the outer lower ranges of the Andes ; finally, there are no very great differences of temperature. It is these factors which pre-eminently cause the surface weathering of stones. Their absence may leave a (well-polished) surface practically unimpaired. Furthermore, the Calendar Gate, as well as the other buildings of the main culture strata of Tiahuanaco have not always been exposed to the weather.

For, as we know, Tiahuanaco became submerged when the Inter-Andean Sea of the Highest Level was formed. The never-finished, public and private, sacred and secular, edifices of the city stayed under water for a long time, till the ebbing of the girdle-tide, of which the Inter-Andean Sea of the Highest Level formed a communicating part. That is why many of the remains are still found to be covered with a firmly adhering, thin layer of a very fine hard limestone. This tufa-like incrustation may have protected the sculptures themselves against the attack of the weather, when they eventually re-emerged. Only the protective incrustation weathered and partly disappeared again. (No tufa-layer is provable on the Calendar Gate, but the monumental stairway of the Temple of Kalasasaya shows it very distinctly.)

One more thing seems to have furthered the preservation of the Calendar sculpture. As the back of the gateway is rather badly weathered while its front is only slightly attacked, it may be assumed that it has been lying face down for very long reaches of time, perhaps for nearly all its existence.[73] None of the early chroniclers or travellers who visited the site seems to mention this by far the most impressive monument of Tiahuanaco. Notices about it first appear in the early part of the Nineteenth Century. Perhaps it had been found by someone prospecting and digging for 'treasure'[74] and was then raised up by someone who was interested in it, probably from a purely utilitarian point of view. For a smaller gate with a sculptured frieze which is a 'continuation' of the lowest part of the Calendar Gate (i.e. the line of Twelfth-heads) was removed from the precincts of Kalasasaya some time ago, and set up as an entrance-gate for a now disused burial-ground of the present village of Tiahuanaco (cf. Diagram 6). The only logical place for the great Calendar Gate is a certain point near the centre of the Sun Temple of Kalasasaya. There, originally, it may have been lying face down, and from there it has probably been removed. During the process of raising and transporting, the monolith, which weighs some ten tons, seems to have broken in two (cf. Diagrams 12 and 13), and the venture was abandoned. The edges of the break are not weathered which proves that the damage must be of comparatively recent date.

A word more about the original position of the Calendar Gate. It was found dumped near the north-western corner of the Temple of Kalasasaya. Someone tried to raise it and fit the two fragments together, but the Gate soon collapsed again because it was not placed on a firm foundation. Only in 1910 did the Bolivian authorities provide the latter. The Calendar Gate must have originally stood astride the central axis of the Temple of Kalasasaya, on the highest elevation, near the centre of the temple area. (Cf. the Plan of Tiahuanaco, Diagram 10.) A foundation slab has recently been unearthed there which must have been provided for something 'very specially important', nay 'unique', because it consists of a trachyte, a stone which has been exclusively used at this one spot in all the prehistoric metropolis; indeed, it must have been brought from very far, since up till now no find-place of trachyte has yet been discovered in the Tiahuanaco region. The most important and unique object is, without the slightest doubt, the Calendar Gate. Its carved side probably faced west. From a certain point a little to the west of the Calendar Gate, therefore, the Sun would have appeared to rise approximately above the respective heads at the beginning of each Twelfth.[74a] As the sculptured calendar pictured the course of the Sun from solstice to solstice, it showed the Sun, so to speak, the course it should take. If this 'magical coercion' element in our explanation be not allowed, then the sculptor merely copied from the Sun its annual journey in the heavens. From the portal of the pylon, no doubt, the necessary astronomical observations were made to determine the four chief points of the year, the two equinoxes, and the two solstices, and—judging from the pictorialism of the calendar sculpture—certain ceremonial and ritual observances were enacted there also. (Cf. Note 52.) Viewed from the gateway, the Sun rose exactly over the northern corner pillar of an inner enclosure—which, luckily, has been preserved *in situ*—at the winter solstice ('June'). At the summer solstice ('December') it rose exactly over the southern corner pillar, which has not been preserved but whose position can easily be determined from the other remaining pillars of the inner enclosure. At the time of the spring ('September') and autumn ('March') equinoxes, the Sun rose exactly over the monumental east portal of the Temple of Kalasasaya (whose detailed ground-plan has been preserved, hewn into its foundation slabs). It is likely that its great megalithic flight of steps had been specially designed in honour of the Sun.

In an earlier part of this book we said that the remains of the Tiahuanaco of the 'classical period' were probably rediscovered by settlers who were looking for a site likely to be safe from a great and extensive inundation of the lower-lying territories which they were expecting to happen. Though the suddenness of the 'capture cataclysm' of our present Moon probably prevented the actual settlement of the Tiahuanaco Region by great masses of refugees, it may be expected that a few did settle there. It may therefore be argued that it was they who made the Calendar gateway. The sculpture, therefore, might only be about 13,500 years old. Indeed, a similar figure is readily accepted by a number of scientists as the age of the ruins of Tiahuanaco.[75]

In reply to any such endeavours let us put forward the following weighty objection: The symbols of the Sun Gate reveal themselves as eloquent and authoritative chronoglyphs only when we allow them to speak for a certain period towards the end of the Aeon of the Predecessor of our Moon, and for this period exclusively; if this interpretation is not allowed, the carvings on the Sun-Gate can be regarded merely as curiously involved ornaments. For the establishment of that Calendar could never have been effected at the Beginning of the Age of Luna. The year then had practically the same number of days as now, because the shock of the capture, great though it was and terrible though its consequences were, could not have tampered very appreciably with the speed of rotation which the Earth had been given by the tidal urge of the former Satellite in the last stages of its existence, and by the breakdown impacts. If anything at all, Luna may have slightly retarded the rotation of our planet, and made the day a fraction longer again.

In a bold thought-experiment we have linked the Calendar of the Sun Temple of Kalasasaya at Tiahuanaco with the ancient strandline of the Inter-Andean Sea of the Intermediate Level whose waters filled the harbours of the mysterious city and its canals. We have linked it with that strandline whose most significant feature is its rise, with relation to the ocean-level, towards the north of Tiahuanaco, and its fall towards the south of that city. After the foregoing it would appear as if the most fertile—though admittedly the most revolutionary—standpoint to take up is to accept the voice now set echoing from the Calendar Gate and the evidence of the slanting strandline, and hence, also, Hoerbiger's Theory of Satellites, which alone is able to link these facts, to fill them with meaning, and to make them all speak freely and clearly. If what we call the 'voice of experience', which says that such ancient monuments 'cannot' exist, tries to speak against these facts and findings, we shall have to silence this voice; instead, we shall have to let the 'voice of the new evidence' speak without hindrance, and build up a new 'experience' upon its counsels. If we listen patiently and carefully to what the Calendar and the strandline tell us, all doubts, which are really quite legitimate, will eventually be quashed.

This is not an easy way out of a difficulty: *It is the only possible way leading to the solution of the enigmas of Tiahuanaco.*

But could the Calendar Gate not be a copy of a lost original? Or the copy of a copy?

No! For there speaks such an original mind out of this calendar sculpture, the mind both of the ingenious deviser of that time-chart, and the mind of the masterful sculptor who translated the idea into stone. The copyist, therefore, would have been a mere soulless drudge who spent incessant labour upon the huge slab of glass-hard andesite to fashion the obstinate material into mazes of difficult meanders and a profusion of intricate shapes whose thus-ness he could not have in the least understood.

It is improbable, nay, it is impossible, that the Calendar sculpture of Tiahuanaco is an original creation of what is practically yesterday. The evidence given distinctly and insistently by the grand piece of sculpture is too strong. For among the chronoglyphs we find at least one animal which does not occur now anywhere near Tiahuanaco: The Flying Fish. And we find among them also at least one animal which has been extinct since Tertiary Times: the Toxodon.[76]

As regards the toxodon, palaeontologists say that no living man can have seen that peculiar, exclusively South American animal. Nevertheless the inhabitants of Tiahuanaco must have been quite familiar with this queer 'living fossil', which was already very much 'out of date' in the Tertiary Period. They seem to have regarded the big placid grass-eater as a sacred animal, a relic of the 'sunny' world of the times before the impending cataclysm, for it is frequently depicted with a white disk, the symbol of the Sun, attached to its neck, or superimposed on its nose. If this portraiture is not allowed as a proof of its existence at that time, then the toxodon bones which are found in the alluvial soil of Tiahuanaco and its neighbourhood, together with human remains, pottery, worked stone, and other evidences of culture, certainly must.

164

THE CALENDAR OF KALASASAYA

As regards the flying fish—such delicate fishes live only in the warm waters of the tropical seas, while cold Lake Titicaca is situated in the bleak uplands of the Andes, and has been there since the end of the Tertiary Age. The sculptor of the Calendar of Tiahuanaco must have known the flying fish very well to use it so aptly, and so humorously, for the characterization of the two 'extra' days of the Tiahuanaco Year which otherwise would have upset his beautifully balanced '$(1 + 11) \times 24$' scheme, but which in this way actually help to accentuate that balance. (Cf. Diagram 23.) For they come 'flown onto', and stick to, the day haloes of the Sixth and Eighth Twelfths, just as flying fishes may drop down nowadays onto a vessel cruising in the tropical seas.[77] (Cf. Diagrams 17 and 18.) But also the inhabitants of the Andinian Metropolis must have been well enough acquainted with that aquatic animal and its astounding aeronautical habits to understand and appreciate the clever joke of the sculptor's.

Of course, someone may say that the pictograph of the flying fish proves, if anything, that the Calendar sculpture was really the work of the refugees who had formerly lived at the Pacific sea-shore in tropical latitudes, but had had to leave their paradisial homes—for fear of the capture cataclysm of Luna, if the picture drawn by Hoerbiger's Cosmological Theory be allowed, or for some undiscoverable and unexplainable reason, if it be not—and emigrated to the bleak Meseta of the Andes with its thin air, cold water, and scanty vegetation; that, when they built their tremendous megalithic metropolis there, they also built a Calendar Temple; and that they put the flying fish onto its principal gateway in continual and characteristical commemoration of their former happy home. The fish, so to speak, was to remind them continually of the warmth of the waters of their former sea. But such trends of thought are quite idle; nay, they are absolutely unreasonable.

Then there are those who, quite correctly, link the slanting shore-lines of the Tiahuanaco Asylum, and elsewhere in the Andes, with the flying fish, but who—not knowing, or not

165

accepting, Hoerbiger's Theory—say that the city, built at a time when the mighty back-bone of South America had not yet been raised out of the Ocean, was therefore situated at sea-level, and that the ocean-waters in that latitude were warm enough for flying fish, as well as hippocampi, etc. We need hardly waste a thought upon the idea of such a terrific uplift of perhaps 17,000 feet[78] since Tertiary Times. The adherents of the uplift hypothesis have one point which is in our favour, though; they see no difficulty in attributing an exceedingly remote date to the ruins.

The only possibility of a natural and unforced solution which remains, therefore, is that which our Theory of Satellites offers: the girdle-tide caused by the approaching Predecessor of our present Moon. Then the close Satellite drew the waters together into the tropical latitudes in the form of a flood-belt (cf. Diagram 2) which, in the latitude of Tiahuanaco, reached a height of about 12,600 feet (reckoned from the present sea-level) at the time when the Calendar was made, but reached about 700 feet more subsequently, when the city was submerged. Nearer the equator, where the axis of the girdle-tide was situated,[79] the waters reached a greater height; farther to the south of Tiahuanaco (and, of course, also to the north of the equator) they were lower. Hence the peculiar slant of the ancient strand-lines in the Inter-Andean Basin. (Cf. Diagram 11.) When these conditions prevailed Tiahuanaco was actually situated 'at sea-level'. Its position was even more 'tropical' then than it would be now if it were situated at sea-level in the same latitude (16° 57′ S.); partly that was because of the air-tide-ring which at that time had also been piled up by the close Satellite in the tropics and had increased the atmospheric 'blanket' effect; and partly because it seems very likely that at the time of its floreat Tiahuanaco was situated appreciably nearer the (then) equator. That was the time when flying fish lived there. They, and probably also other forms of more delicate marine life, died when, after the end of the Satellite, the waters of the ocean suddenly fell some 17,000 feet at the least, and the dense, warm air-ring flowed off too, and the Andean Plateau, so to speak, 'shot' up into the cold rarefied atmosphere of great heights.

With this we close our discussion of the problems of Tiahuanaco. Whatever more tangible results this book may eventually realize, the Reader will agree that the preceding chapters have allowed many unexpected glimpses into a world that was hitherto unknown, and revealed one of the ancient homes of man and its great capital which was built before the cosmically caused Great Flood scourged our planet. This reconstruction of a lost age of our Earth was made possible by Hans Hoerbiger's Cosmological Theory of the terrestrial Satellites. To this great Viennese and his work we owe our thanks.

Postscript

AN IMPORTANT TASK

The literature about Tiahuanaco, from the first Spanish chroniclers who set foot on the Altiplano to the travellers of recent times who have visited the site, is not inconsiderable. However, with the exception of the writings of Posnansky, Bennett, Stuebel, and Kiss (cf. Bibliography) the observations of the authors are mostly superficial and frequently incorrect.

Many of the visitors of Tiahuanaco were men of great learning, some even experienced explorers. Yet it is one of the major puzzles of modern archaeology that none of them should have found it worth while to study the ruins in detail, leisurely, and systematically. For all of them are of opinion that Tiahuanaco is a most interesting and important site, deserving thorough and undivided attention. Neither Bolivia nor Peru has hitherto produced a son sufficiently awake to devote his life to the exploration of the archaeological remains in these countries, or a Government interested enough to appropriate adequate funds for that work.

The most notable explorer of Tiahuanaco is easily Professor Arthur Posnansky, who has lived among, or near, the ruins for several decades[80] and who has done most valuable work both by recording photographically most of the remains and by making detailed surveys of the site. His work is all the more commendable because it has hardly ever found the recognition that it deserves.

Because of this almost universal lack of sustained interest, Tiahuanaco is probably the most mangled and most ruthlessly pilfered site known to archaeology. The large-scale destruction of the remains by speculating builders from the time of the Conquista to the time of the construction of the La Paz-

169

Guaqui railway has been followed recently by the no less vandalistic petty thieving of the inhabitants of the Tiahuanaco region.

In these latter years, whenever a passing traveller did a few days' digging among the ruins and uncovered some worked stones, they were stolen overnight if they were small enough to be carried without inconvenience, and thus lost, practically beyond recovery, since there is hardly any authority in Bolivia that would put itself out to reclaim them.

It is somewhat surprising that none of the great Scientific Foundations has hitherto sponsored an expedition to Tiahuanaco to save whatever there is still to be saved. There can be no doubt that astonishing finds can still be made there, since up till now nearly all attempts to dig on the site have been of the most desultory kind, hardly amounting to more than a scratching of the surface.[81] It is hoped that this serious omission will be remedied at no very distant date.

And the writer also hopes sincerely that a number of persons who are still possessed of some means in these times will put sums at the disposal of a Tiahuanaco Exploration Society, yet to be formed. Even so small a sum as ten thousand pounds —that is, one hundred times one hundred pounds (or two hundred times fifty pounds, etc.)—would allow a year's very intensive field-work by a group of interested scientists assisted by a gang of native labourers.

An expedition to Tiahuanaco would have to undertake chiefly the following work:

to acquire far-reaching concessions for exploration from the Bolivian (and Peruvian) government(s), with full power to protect the site(s) during excavation to prevent the looting, or displacing, of the material found. (Posnansky's suggestion of acquiring the whole region by buying out the villagers of Tiahuanaco would be well worth considering);

to make a careful survey of the region, by air as well as by land;

to make a new and detailed survey of the various ancient strandlines in the Altiplano and elsewhere;

to survey all the ruin-fields known and yet to be discovered;

to establish the level of all the sites;

to trace the ground-plans, etc., of all the ruins, and the layout of the sites;

to survey all the blocks still *in situ* as to shape, measurements, weight, material, etc.;

to make an inventory on similar lines of all the looted blocks which can be ascertained in private houses, churches, etc., and to acquire these as far as deemed important;

to lift up all gateways still lying face down, as well as certain slabs, etc., in order to inspect the other side;

to make a catalogue of all genuine Tiahuanaco material (especially that of the 'classical' period) in public and private collections;

to undertake careful and systematic digging, chiefly down to the level of the Tiahuanaco of the 'classic' period;

to compile an atlas of all ornamental (possibly ideographic) devices on sculptures, pottery, metal implements, etc.;

to gather myths and folklore among aboriginal tribes of the Tiahuanaco region; and

to publish all results of the work undertaken.

The result of this work of exploration would also help the theory advanced in this book to be accepted—or rejected. At any rate, it would bring forth quantities of exceedingly valuable material about that most unique and hitherto so sadly neglected culture of Tiahuanaco which would benefit many branches of science.

Bibliography

M. E. de Rivero and J. J. von Tschudi: Antigüedades Peruanas. 1851.

E. G. Squier: Peru. Incidents of Travel and Exploration in the Land of the Incas. 1877.

G. Chaworth Musters: Notes on Bolivia (Journal of the Royal Geographical Society, vol. 47). 1877.

R. Inwards: The Temple of the Andes. 1884.

A. Stuebel (and M. Uhle): Die Ruinenstaette von Tiahuanaco im Hochlande des Alten Perú. 1892.

I. M. Neveu-Lemaire: Les Lacs des Hauts-Plateaux de l'Amérique du Sud. 1906.

V. Huot: Géographie des Hauts-Plateaux des Andes. 1908.

Sir Clements R. Markham: The Land of the Incas (Geographical Journal, vol. xxxvii, No. 4). 1910.

A. Posnansky: El Clima del Altiplano y la Extensión del Lago Titicaca con relación á Tihuanacu en épocas prehistóricas. 1911.

—— Tihuanacu y la Civilisación Prehistórica en el Altiplano andino. 1911.

—— Guía general ilustrada para la investigación de los monumentos prehistóricos de Tihuanacu. 1912.

Th. A. Joyce: South American Archaeology. 1912.

H. Hoerbiger and Ph. Fauth: Glazialkosmogonie. 1913.

A. Posnansky: El Signo Escalonado en las ideografías americanas con especial referencia á Tihuanacu. 1913.

—— Una Metrópoli Prehistórica en la América del Sur. 1914.

—— Kulturvorgeschichtliches und die astronomische Bedeutung des Grossen Sonnentempels von Tihuanacu in Bolivia. (Proceedings of the 21st Int. Congress of Americanists). 1924.

Enciclopedia Universal Ilustrada Europeo-Americana. 1928.

BIBLIOGRAPHY

P. A. Means: Ancient Civilizations of the Andes. 1931.

W. C. Bennett: Excavations at Tiahuanaco. 1934.

—— Excavations in Bolivia. 1936.

H. S. Bellamy: Moons, Myths, and Man. 1936.

E. Kiss: Das Sonnentor von Tihuanaku. 1937.

A. Posnansky: Tiahuanacu, the Cradle of American Man. 1945.

MAPS

Régions des Hauts-Plateaux de l'Amérique du Sud. 1:750.000. 1903.

Mapa Aproximado de Bolivia. 1:250.000. 1933.

Mapa General de Bolivia. 1:1,000.000. 1934.

Notes

¹ Titicaca, which may mean Puma-Rock, is really only the name of one of the islands in the lake, whose actual ancient appellation, now never used, is Chuquivitu, or Chucuito in a simplified Spanish spelling. The Quechua words *Chuqui-vitu* may approximately be rendered as 'Racing Waters', an appellation which may contain a memory of the water catastrophes which happened in the Altiplano in times of old.

² Difference in level between Lake Titicaca and Lake Poöpo only 455 feet.

³ Difference in level between Lake Poöpo and Lake Coipasa only 20 feet.

⁴ Because of the peculiar slant of the level of the waters at that period, as shown on Diagram 11, the Inter-Andean Sea of the Highest Level was probably in effective communication with the outer ocean through the Uyuni Gap only occasionally and for short periods.

⁵ The lunar orbital undulations are so shallow that even the new-moon arcs are still concave relative to the Sun. This is, of course, only a very rough description, for in reality the system Terra : Luna revolves round a common gravitational centre which is situated about three-quarters of a terrestrial radius outside the Earth's centre. Hence also the Earth's orbit, i.e. the path of its centre, is actually a complicated, undulating (and because of the orbital diminution also helicoidal) curve.

⁶ From various considerations (which cannot be entered into here) it appears likely that the former Satellite was somewhat—possibly even considerably—smaller than Luna; hence its influence, distance regarded as being the same, will have been proportionately smaller; or, in other words, the former Satellite must have been proportionately nearer to wield a similar influence. (Cf. also Note 60.)

⁷ Cf. the case made out in the present writer's books, *Moons, Myths, and Man, The Book of Revelation is History*, and *In the Beginning God*, all published by Faber & Faber Ltd.

⁸ Abyssinia and Tibet have hardly been explored prehistorically yet; Andinia is only very superficially known; in Mexico alone prehistorians seem hitherto to have taken some interest.

⁹ Other remains showing the characteristic style of the 'First Period' have been discovered near Taraco, Lloquepaya, Copacapana, Cusijata, Jesús de Machaca, Escoma, Carabuco, Patapatani, Pariti, Lukurmata, and elsewhere in this region, but have hardly been explored yet.

¹⁰ The Precession, a slow wobbling movement of the Earth's axis, is due

NOTES

to extra-terrestrial forces (chiefly the gravitation of the Moon and the Sun) acting upon the equatorial 'bulge' of our planet. In the days of the former Satellite this wobbling must have been much quicker and more pronounced, and probably also subjected to rather spasmodic changes, because of the greater flattening of our globe then, and because of the nearness and orbital speed of the Satellite—factors which enhanced its levering action. This precessional wobble was eventually necessarily followed by a slight shift of the terrestrial axis.

The actuality of the precessional wobble and of the small shift of the Poles which came in its train is proved, and its extent (about 4° 30') shown, by the orientation of the buildings of the First Period which is distinctly different from that of the edifices of the Second Period. (Cf. buildings B, C, D, and western F, and edifices A, E, and eastern F, on Diagram 10, p. 53.) The Fortress of Akapana belongs to both periods; its vast size made re-orientation impracticable.

[11] That is why the water-catastrophe is regarded as having been caused by the breakdown of a great glaciation, and why these ruins are usually regarded as 'pre-glacial' even by scientists who are otherwise not ready to concede a great age to the culture remains in the Andinian Asylum.

[12] A free rendering. According to the Viennese scientist, Rudolf Falb, the meaning of Ttahua-ntin-Suyu is 'Four Cardinal-Point Country'. The literal translation of the three Quechua words is: *ttahua*, four; *ntin*, together; *suyu*, region.

[13] Andesite takes its place in Mohs's mineralogical scale of hardness between orthoclase (6) and quartz (7). It is a greyish, or greenish-grey, igneous rock consisting of microscopic hornblende, biotite, diopside, and apatite, crystals embedded in a matrix of volcanic glass.

[14] This volcano is now extinct, but it may well have been active at the time when Tiahuanaco was built, or the volcanic origin of the mountain must have been somehow inferred, for its name, in Aymara, means something like 'Rock with a Vent'.

[15] Worked andesite blocks of a weight up to 65 tons have been found. In their unworked or roughly squared state they must have been considerably heavier. (Worked sandstone blocks of the classic period even weigh up to 100 tons.)

[16] This may allow us eventually to establish the length of the Tiahuanaco 'inch' and 'foot'. (From numerous measurements of the remains of the Temple of Kalasasaya Posnansky has already inferred a mensural unit equalling almost exactly $4\frac{1}{2}$ feet.) The measuring system of the Tiahuanacans, both as regards lengths and angles, must have been highly developed: for all the heavy intricately shaped blocks and their complicated counterparts surely could not have been made to fit, and to fit exactly, by the laborious method of constantly matching, removing, altering, and replacing.

175

NOTES

[17] Thus the Mapa Aproximado de Bolivia, 1933.—The exact location of Tiahuanaco does not seem to be absolutely certain. According to the *Enciclopedia Universal Europeo-Americana*, ed. 1928, the situation of Tiahuanaco is 16° 32′ 43″ S., 68° 20′ 35″ W. Posnansky, a very careful authority, gives the location 16° 34′ 54″ S., 68° 49′ 30″ W., for the Temple of Kalasasaya.

[18] This height actually refers to the ancient water-level of the Inter-mediate Inter-Andean Sea, measured at the harbour-walls of the pre-historic city, an important 'zero-point'.

[19] *Their* 'world': the Andinian Refuge.

[20] Another peculiar 'echo' is worth recording. That part of Lake Titicaca which extends to the north of Tiahuanaco is called the Lagoon of Huiñay-marca. This is a strange name to give to a sheet of water, for it means, in the language of the Aymara, something like 'ever(lasting) city'. The only possible explanation is that this name harks back to the time when the 'sacred' region of Tiahuanaco was a peninsula in the waters of the Inter-Andean Sea of the Intermediate Level, that it originally referred to that territory, and that, when the memory of the true meaning had faded, the name was transferred to the remains of that Sea.

[21] Originally the description 'decaying Moon' referred to the disinteg-rating former satellite. The ancient mythological report of the actual 'dying' was probably reinterpreted after the capture of Luna, when the remarkable phenomenon of the 'waning' of the new Satellite was observed, and had to be magically counteracted.

[21a] This doorway has recently been dismantled and fifteen of its bigger constituents reassembled into a doorway of slightly different form.

[21b] Only this and another window which closely resembles it have been found hitherto. It is not known where exactly in the Temple of Kalasasaya they were used, or intended to be used, but their exceptional design suggests that they must have been set into the wall of a very 'sacred' *cella*-like inmost sanctuary of the Temple.

At Puma Punku two rectangular monolithic windows have been found, one resembling the gateway shown in Diagram 5, with lintel, jambs, and sill in one piece, and another resembling the gateways in Diagrams 6, 12 and 13, consisting of lintel and jambs only. Their openings measure about 25 by 15 inches.

[22] The name Kalasasaya means something like 'Stone-Stead', or 'Stone-Pile', which aptly describes the megalithic style of its remains. (Cf. also Note 37.)

[23] Akapana was definitely a citadel, or acropolis, as is also stressed by its strategic position and lay-out. Aka-khapana, in Aymara, means 'in this place (it is) where one rules'.

[24] 'Puma Punku', in Aymara, means 'Puma, or Silver Lion, Gate'; but the edifice should perhaps be more correctly called 'Huma Punku',

176

NOTES

'Water Gate', since its gates opened directly onto two harbour basins. The name 'Tunca Punku', by which this site is sometimes locally known, means 'Ten Gates', and may contain an echo regarding the original lay-out of the edifice. It certainly seems to have had quite a number of entrances.

[25] Some explorers of the site of Tiahuanaco are of opinion that the 'canal' was, at most, only a 'dry moat', and hence will not concede that the peculiar rectangular depressions near the ruins were once actual docks or harbour-basins. But the proofs in favour of our assertion that Tiahuanaco was once a harbour-town are stronger than any of the objections put forward by more superficial observers.

Firstly: there is a rapid fall in level from the edge of the territory which bears culture-remains to the floor of the territory which we say was covered by the waters of the Inter-Andean Sea of the Intermediate Level. The difference in level is about 35 feet north of Tiahuanaco proper, and even 60 feet near Puma Punku.

Secondly: while the soil of the territory which we say was above the water level contains numerous ceramic fragments and other remains, the former sea-bottom yields practically nothing but the stone-rings with which the fishermen of that time used to weight their nets.

Thirdly: the 'dumps' of roughly squared stone-blocks (cf. pp. 38 foll.) are found only on territory which formerly was sea-bottom.

Moreover, the 'dry moat' must have been a water-bearing canal because the great sewer, which drained the overflow of the pond on the platform of the 'fortress' of Akapana, discharged into it. (Cf. Diagram 10.)

[26] Umayo, from the Aymara, *Huma Hayo*, means something like 'Bitter (i.e. Salt) Water'. As the water of that lake is absolutely sweet now the name must contain an echo of the time when, in contrast to other lakes of the region, it held some of the water of the Inter-Andean Sea of the Intermediate Level with which it then communicated.

[27] From the fact that wild potato plants are found exclusively in the region about Lake Titicaca it is argued that the original home of the potato was situated there. Whether the potato was known to, and cultivated by, the Tiahuanacans we cannot say. The potatoes at present grown there are not derived from the native plants, but from tubers imported 'recently' from Europe (and ultimately, therefore, of 'North American' extraction). Yet it is interesting to note that practically all members of the family Solanaceae are of 'tropical' origin. Hence the wild potato plants with their diminutive (practically inedible) tubers may well be survivors (possibly stunted) from the time when that region was really tropical not only as to latitudinal situation but also as to climate.

[28] So in the region called Managasha, the 'Holy Land', a high-lying area belonging to the Coptic Church. There also cave-dwellings are found. Abyssinia has hardly been touched by the archaeologist yet.

[29] Practically all the numerous volcanoes of the Central Andes, no matter whether active or extinct, date from the latest stage of the Tertiary Age or from the early part of the Pleistocene Period.

[30] There is a considerable number of caves in the Cordilleras in the region of the Inter-Andean Asylum. They are practically unexplored, but some are known to contain ancient human remains and cultural deposits.

[31] Direct evidences of this sudden rarefaction and 'change of climate' do not yet seem to have been found, or noticed, in the Altiplano. But it should be mentioned that near Bogotá, in Colombia, situated only little below the level of Tiahuanaco, there is the so-called 'Field of the Giants', an extensive plain covered with the bones of 'mastodons'. It is evident that these prehistoric elephants were surprised by a sudden elevation of their habitat and grazing ground, and perished from the cold, the sudden rarefaction of the air, and the lack of food caused by the consequent destruction of the tropical vegetation.

There is also an interesting, and important, contribution from mythology. The Aymaras tell in one of their little-known myths that in ancient times the mightiest of all gods, *Khunu Titi Huirakocha* ('Snow— or Ice—Puma Earth-Maker') punished a wicked people by flinging a coat of snow (or ice) over their country, which made life very hard also for those who lived in the neighbourhood and had not been guilty of any trespass. This myth contains, if anything, a most distinct memory of the great glaciation which started when the Andes 'rose' at the end of the great cataclysm of the predecessor of our Moon.

[32] We must remember that in the moonless age which followed the end of the former Satellite the oceans were considerably lower in tropical latitudes and higher in the polar ones. Only when Luna, our present Moon, was acquired by our Earth as a companion, did its gravitational pull draw the waters again slightly into the tropics, and hold them there in a shallow permanent tide, the beginnings of a new girdle-tide.

[33] The sun is usually depicted by a *white* disk on the polychrome pottery of Tiahuanaco, and its determinative symbol is a harmless-looking animal which has been interpreted as the toxodon.—Occasionally a very small white disk, or circle, is depicted on vases, sometimes with a gentle-looking llama-like animal as a determinator. This has been taken to symbolize the planet Venus. However, viewing it from the standpoint of Hoerbiger's Theory, I venture the guess that the tiny white disk is the symbol of the *planet Luna* which must at that time have been the most conspicuous heavenly body visible in the night-sky and may at times have actually appeared as a distinct disk.

[34] Cf. the present author's book *Moons, Myths, and Man*, pp. 146–7.

[35] The writer is convinced that in this region one of the 'original' languages of mankind was spoken. It was most probably a blend of different older elements. There are certain definite and very striking

connexions of Aymara, Quechua, etc., with the Aryan and Semitic languages.

[36] None of the prehistoric human remains found in the Tiahuanaco area show any 'primitive' traits. This has been cited as a decisive argument against the comparatively great age which we attribute to them. But there is no conceivable reason to believe that *all* men were pithecoid, cultureless, shambling brutes, say, five thousand generations ago. Indeed, many anthropologists now remove the neanderthaloid sub-men to a time at least thirty thousand generations from us.

[37] Kalasasaya is not the name of the Sun Temple of Tiahuanaco, but merely a local term which means something like 'Stone-Stead' (Aymara *ccala*, stone; and, probably, *sayani*, stand up). The appellation is thus almost synonymous with, and as descriptive as, our 'Stonehenge'. Though extensively used the expression 'Sun Temple *of* Kalasasaya' is, therefore, not a very correct one.

[38] Before the door-opening and the niches and cornices at the back, as well as the sculptures on the front of the gate had been made, the block or slab of rock must have weighed considerably more than twelve tons.

[39] But for an unlucky chance the Calendar Gate of Kalasasaya might be one of the treasures of the British Museum. The Viennese University Professor Rudolf Falb tells that he had found an interested person who was ready to pay for the transport of the gateway to London, to the British Museum, if he (Falb) could get the Bolivian authorities to permit its removal. But owing to the war between Bolivia and Chile in 1878 Falb had to leave the country before his negotiations were successful. If the gateway had been removed to the British Museum it would have been spared the wanton mutilation of its carvings to which it is continuously exposed by stone-throwing or pistol-shooting local vandals. Also, if the gateway—or at least a cast of it—were in London the Site of Tiahuanaco would not be the Cinderella of archaeological exploration which it is, for the interest and curiosity of both scientists and patrons alike would be powerfully stimulated.

[39a] Less than a mile from the Temple of Kalasasaya, in the ruin-complex of Puma Punku, the badly shattered fragments of at least four other monolithic gateways of practically the same dimensions as the Calendar Gate are to be found, half-buried in 'alluvial' soil. They were all lying 'face down', but quite recently at least one of the gates was raised to examine the front. It was found to be covered with a meander frieze somewhat similar to that of the Calendar Gate. Posnansky believes that Puma Punku was the 'Temple of the Moon' of the Tiahuanacans, just as Kalasasaya was their 'Temple of the Sun'. He is probably right, as the meander of Puma Punku shows fish-heads where that of Kalasasaya has condor-heads. Unfortunately the carvings are too obliterated to make out really helpful details, and the whole meander-line is too fragmentary to allow even a tentative general description or interpretation. The 'faces'

which have been preserved have a halo of only 16 symbols, for instance. Maybe the other gateways will reveal more details to allow an analysis.

[39b] The fragments of the four gateways at Puma Punku show 'architectural' ornaments—niches, cornices, etc.—which are in all respects similar to those on the back of the Calendar Gate. Moreover, these fragments show a similar damage to the niches, and at the base.

[40] As far as can be established they were always mere arbitrary general subdivisions of the year in accordance with the formerly far-prevailing duodecimal system. The number of the 'months' may have been chosen for some 'mystical' reason, possibly for the same reason for which the ecliptic, or zodiac, was divided into twelve parts.

[41] Cf. Old English *wice*, exchange; Old High German *wehsal*, change.— Hence there were originally—in ancient Teutonic times—only two 'weeks' in every lunar month, one beginning with the New Moon, and the other beginning with the Full Moon. The term 'fortnight' contains the echo of a memory of that time. The seven-day 'week', or 'sennight', is of non-Teutonic (Semitic and Roman) origin. It was probably originally based on the 'seven planets' known to the ancients, not on the phase-changes of the Moon.

[42] The writer here follows in essentials the relative passages in the valuable work by Edmund Kiss: *Das Sonnentor von Tihuanaku*.

[43] To have an absolute standard of comparing time we are asked in this examination to regard the 'hour' as an absolute unit of time, not produced by dividing the 'day' of each period, i.e. the time of one complete rotation of the Earth, into 24 equal parts, but as being the time marked by an ideally correct clock of our days when its pendulum, or balance-wheel, swings a requisite number of times.

[44] Most probably the different general divisions of the calendar sculpture were originally painted, and the individual symbols picked out, in different colours. The Tiahuanacans were very fond of bold, if occasionally somewhat sombre, pigments, as may be inferred from their pottery. (As to the colour schemes of the Tiahuanacans cf. also Diagram 3 facing p. 36.)

[45] While it is impossible to say how far these extensions were continued it appears likely that they were not continued indefinitely. Most probably there was another panel of 15 figures each on either side of the main panels, which had an ornamental purpose only. The line of eleven heads may have been repeated ornamentally once, or several times, to the right and left of the calendarial line. (Cf. also text of Diagram 6 on p. 47, and the reference on p. 161.)

[46] The objects the figure of the First Twelfth holds in its hands are usually described as 'sceptres'. Yet it is much more likely that the object grasped in the right hand is a 'spear-thrower', and the object held in the left hand a 'quiver with (two) spears'. Also the winged

NOTES

anthropoid and ornithoid figures on the 'panels' to the right and left of
the figure of the First Twelfth (Diagram 20) grasp the one or the other of
these ceremonial or rank-indicating objects in their hands.

[47] Because of the phenomenon of the Precession of the Equinoxes the
Southern Autumnal Equinox of that time, if they had used the Gregorian
Calendar, did *not* occur on 'June 22nd', of course—but the nicety is
of no practical importance; for we compare here the various cardinal
points of the Calendar of Kalasasaya with those of our own only for the
sake of gaining a more plastic and readily grasped picture of that Time
Chart.

[48] The uniform red tint in which the symbols in Diagrams 14–19 have
been printed has only been used to show the haloes up more clearly.
While we do not know what colours were actually used the following
guess, based upon similar symbols depicted on polychromous vases, shall
be put forward. The disks were practically certainly yellow, as were also
the puma 'noses'; the toxodon 'noses' were white; the condor-heads may
have been painted a brownish-red and their beaks a light olive; the eyes
of all symbols (again judging from vase-paintings) were probably depicted
half black and half white, the black half (i.e. the pupil) being in the
direction the animal is looking. The colours of the other symbols cannot be
determined with any certainty.

At the occasion of the publication of this new edition I want to confess
to stupid mistakes I made when drawing Diagrams 14 and 16, and the
Tenth Twelfth of Diagram 23, from a rubbing. The elements of the
meander band round these heads (non-numerical symbol No. 6) ought
to 'turn' in the same direction as those in the band round the 'heads'
depicted in Diagrams 15, 17, and 18. These meander-bands are probably
purely ornamental. (Cf. also pp. 118f.) Still, unconfessed, the mistakes
might mislead readers who might want to co-operate in finding out
further secrets of the Tiahuanaco Calendar.

[49] That is, 'Condor Paramount-Chief'. (Philologists should compare
Aymara *mayku* [or *mallku*] and Arabic *malko*, a chief; Hebrew *melech*, a
king.) Many Aymara and Quechua words—too many to dismiss the matter
as merely fortuitous—appear to be related to Aryan and Semitic ones. (Cf.
also Note 35.)

[50] Strictly speaking, only the central piece of the Calendar, which alone
matters, ends there. The chronoglyphs are continued beyond the caesura
indicated by the condor-pointers, but obviously for ornamental purposes
only. (See also pp. 92 f. and Notes 45 and 59.)

[51] Note the peculiar artistic treatment of the two little figures: their
heads and feet are shown in profile while their bodies and arms are depicted in front view, a mannerism familiar from Egyptian art.

[52] It is possible that the pictorialism of the glyphs of the solstitial buglers
indicates that at these times of the year a ceremony was performed at

181

which trumpets were sounded in the Temple of Kalasasaya to 'request the Sun to return' at the time of the winter solstice, and to 'request the Sun to remain' at the summer solstice. The *khuepa*-blower would be an important dignitary at such ceremonies, a supposition which seems to be borne out by the very detailed and careful treatment which the sculptor has accorded to these two little figures.

Possibly also the elaborately dressed figure of the First Twelfth holding out its ceremonial staves like an offering towards the Sun which rose directly opposite it on the New Year's (i.e. Autumn Equinox) Day, points to a similar ceremony performed by a high priest in full robes.

[53] The original calculations relating to this state of affairs (Hoerbiger's 'Stage 24'), dated August 1927, are preserved in the archives of the Hoerbiger Institute in Vienna. A photograph of one of the sheets is printed in Kiss's book, *Das Sonnentor von Tihuanaku*. The discussion of the method Hoerbiger employed, or evolved, is quite beyond the scope of this book.

[54] On other sculptures, and on the painted pottery of Tiahuanaco, the various 'numerical' symbols are evidently used as decorative ornaments only, much as we, for instance, might employ 'crosses', or 'crescents', or 'swastikas', to adorn some object, without wishing to impart a religious or political impression thereby.

[55] On the polychromous pottery of Tiahuanaco the 'determinative' disk is always painted *white* when used in connection with the toxodon: it is then the solar emblem; when it appears in connection with the puma the disk is painted *yellow* and is then determinative of the Satellite. Possibly a similar differentiation was attempted on the calendar sculpture, for there is good reason to suppose that it was originally also made more 'readable' by the use of colour.

[56] Posnansky and Kiss are not quite sure about the toxodon and puma symbols. The former is inclined to call the glyphs with disks for noses, sometimes 'puma' and sometimes 'toxodon' (*huari-huillka*, which means something like 'sacred being of the Sun'), while the latter addresses them collectively as 'toxodons'.

And yet the differentiation is very easy. For the puma is always depicted with the characteristic, big, rounded ear of *felis concolor*, while the toxodon (which is supposed to have had very inconspicuous ears) is always depicted earless; the 'collar' of the puma is different from that of the toxodon; the face of the puma is more square, whereas that of the toxodon is more oblong; the mouth of the puma is curved, while that of the toxodon is straight; the facial expression of the puma is that of an intelligent, furtive, agile hunter, while that of the toxodon is rather that of a slow, placid, heavy grass-cropper; the upper-lip of the puma is adorned with whiskers, while that of the toxodon is smooth.

The various differences mentioned (ear—no ear; whiskers—no whiskers; pointed collar—square collar; etc.) are not due to different artistic treatment necessitated by the sizes of the symbols, for at many places pumas and toxodons of equal size are facing one another (cf. Diagrams 14, 17, and 18: toxodons at the lower corners of the haloes, pumas at the ends of the pedestal).

[57] The 'body' of this 'fish' is only made up of ornamental elements, so as not to distract the attention of the beholder from the important determinative puma-face symbol.

[58] Probably this symbol was actually intended to be read as the last of all.

[59] Like the 'month line' this panel of winged figures is continued to the right and left of the main sculpture, but these parts of the sculpture are only roughly chiselled out. The space occupied by these continuations can be gathered from Diagram 12: three and about one fifth to the left, and two and about one half to the right.

While the 'winged fish' (cf. Note 77) is the depiction of a real living being, the 'winged figures' are mere creations of fancy, like the similarly alate 'angels' ('swift messengers') of Jewish and Christian mythology.

[60] The angle subtended by the Satellite's disk is based on a figure given in the present writer's book *Moons, Myths, and Man*. It is stated there that the Satellite would have subtended about 40° when its distance from the Earth's centre was 1·8 terrestrial radii. From this it is a simple matter to calculate the angle subtended at 5·9 terrestrial radii, the distance of the Satellite at the age of Tiahuanaco. (This figure, 40°, was based upon various calculations and estimates by Hoerbiger, whose mention the compass of this book does not allow. H. S. B.)

[61] If N_l is the number of lunations that took place in N_d days, then the number of times the Satellite crossed the sky, N_s, in that period can be found from the equation:

$$N_l - N_d = N_s$$

It is quite possible that the Tiahuanacans never actually estimated the number of lunations that occurred in the year and recorded the more obvious phenomena, the number of days and the number of passages of the Satellite across the sky, without being aware that the sum of these gave the total number of lunations.

[62] This identification, which was at first only made tentatively, proved to be substantiated in the further course of this investigation. As may be seen from Diagram 22 five of the Satellite's 13 crossings of the sky caused two solar eclipses each. A glance at the figure of the First Twelfth shows that ten of the 19 condors' heads are grouped on its chest, significantly arranged into five pairs.

[63] Only those in the bottom line; in the halo of the First Twelfth different symbols have been used at those key-points, probably for the reason given on p. 135.

[64] This 'puma-headed fish' is also a 'pointer', or reading help, in another

respect: if its head is taken to denote the rising, and its tail the setting, of the Satellite, it becomes evident that the halo symbols of the twelve heads must have been supposed to be 'read' *anti-clockwise*, that is, in the same way in which the successive Twelfths themselves have to be read. The succession of the Twelfths, of course, was determined by the course of the Sun.

[65] Also here we notice the evidently intentional employment of the 'spanning' form of the 'puma-fish' symbol for the characterization of the movement of the Satellite on the 13th day (cf. p. 143).

[66] No attempt has been made to include these variations in sunrise times due to the Equation of Time. This has two separate causes. The first, the Sun's changing declination, can be ignored in the present discussion because it would have been shared by the Satellite. The second is the eccentricity of the Earth's orbit, but, as we do not know the position of the Earth's apses in those days, the slight corrections required for it could not be included. These would not at their highest have amounted to much more than $0 \cdot 1$ T/hours.

[67] It seems more natural to us to begin the year with the vernal equinox. This is probably because the spring appeals to us as a beginning and the autumn as an ending. But this would not be true for people living within the tropics. Even in temperate regions the preference for having the spring at the beginning of the year is by no means universal; the Hebrew year, for example, began with the autumnal equinox. (Posnansky and Kiss regard the First Twelfth as the Vernal Equinox Twelfth. H.S.B.)

[68] From the symbolism of the Calendar may be gathered that the solstices and equinoxes were occasions of special religious and civic festivals. They will always have been calculated exactly by the astronomers of Tiahuanaco and their actual occurrence proclaimed by trumpets and certain ceremonies. Cf. Diagrams 15, 16, and 19. (H. S. B.)

[69] The Equator is not regarded as a line which is always fixed in one position. Orthodox scientists as well as Hoerbiger allow an occasional shift of the Equator, though from different causes, but this is not the place to elaborate upon the problem. Suffice it to say that a position of Tiahuanaco at a latitude of $10°$ S. would tally excellently with the position of the Tertiary Equator, which Hoerbiger deduces, for instance, from the trend of the East African rift valleys, etc. (H. S. B.)

[70] The 'first jewel' in the crowns of the lateral winged figures seems to have served as a sort of determinator. From it may be inferred that T/hours 1-5 may have been called 'condor hours', T/hours 6-10 the 'fish-hours', and T/hours 11-15 the 'toxodon hours'. This classification of the morning, noon, and evening hours applied to the 'day side' only, of course, the figures of the 'night side' being merely mirrored. (H. S. B.)

[71] Mr. Ashton's interpretation allows us to make a guess why the figures of the middle row were given the shape of *watchfully upward-*

gazing condors, and why they carry so great a proportion of satellitic symbols. (Cf. pp. 129f.) Shape, attitude, and load of symbols, are 'pointers' to time, place, and causer, of the eclipses. The 'anthropo-condors', as Posnansky calls them, signify the 'noon-tide' hours, 06·00 to 10·00 T/hours (cf. pp. 138 and 155), when the eclipses would happen 'overhead', and be more awkward to anyone who was out on some task than in the 'morning-tide' and 'evening-tide' hours. (H. S. B.)

72 When enumerating those who have worked to make the Calendar of Kalasasaya give up the secret of its notation the name of Professor Arthur Posnansky ought to be mentioned first and foremost. To his fine mind are due the interpretation of the First and Seventh Twelfths as equinoctial points, and of the Fourth and Tenth Twelfths as solstices; of the twelve heads as subdivisions of the year; and of their manner of counting (Diagram 23); findings which form the sound basis without which our work would have been impossible.

Unfortunately Posnansky has not yet seen his way to follow Hoerbiger, and his disciples. This is why, even in his latest dissertation on the Calendar system of Kalasasaya (in *Tiahuanacu, the Cradle of American Man*) he still owns himself completely nonplussed. He can find absolutely nothing to say about all the manifold wealth of symbolistic groupings, which we have made to speak so eloquently, and, we believe, convincingly, and offers only one guess, namely, that the thirty lateral winged figures represent 'the thirty days of the month of September', as he calls the First Twelfth, which are arranged in 'six weeks of five days each'.

73 The fact that the monolithic gateway is damaged at the *back* at the places where the pins which held it to its foundation were situated (cf. Diagram 13) may be a proof that it was thrown on its *face*, perhaps by an earthquake shock caused by the 'precessional wobble' (cf. p. 68) which made the waters of the girdle-tide rush into the inter-Andean asylum.

74 There are many (for the archaeologist, heartrending) evidences of this form of vandalism. Also a considerable portion of the hill-fortress of Akapana has thus been destroyed by a very thorough treasure seeker. A peculiar obsession of those whom Posnansky, in the bitterness of his heart, calls 'the bestial and savage half-breeds' of the Tiahuanaco region, is that the great blocks and the statues of the classical period were made of a cement and that they contain cores of gold. Hence the continuous chiselling, smashing, and blasting of the beautiful monuments.

74a Indeed, a beautifully worked block, which has been addressed as 'observation pedestal' has been found very near that point. (Alternatively, if the carved side faced east, a pillar or 'statue', standing a certain small distance in front of it would have thrown a shadow approximately upon the respective heads at sunrise.)—Hence, it does not really matter which way the carved side of the Calendar Gate actually faced originally.

[75] Posnansky, and some German astronomers, attribute an age of about 17,000 years to the Tiahuanaco ruins, basing their calculation on the difference in the angle of the obliquity of the ecliptic as revealed by the orientation of the Temple of Kalasasaya, and the present angle. There are two special objections to this procedure. The observed change in the obliquity of the ecliptic may have happened several times, which would add as many times 26,000 years to the supposed age of Tiahuanaco. Secondly, Ashton's interesting calculations seem to prove conclusively that Tiahuanaco was situated considerably more to the north at the time of its floreat, and hence Posnansky, and the others, would have to reconsider their calculations.

[76] Various other sculptures of the classic Tiahuanaco culture period, hence contemporary with the Calendar Gate, as well as the pottery of that time, show pictures of animals which also have long been extinct in that region, such as certain (giant?) crustaceans, batrachidae, and reptiles.

[77] A third 'flying-fish' of somewhat 'abbreviated' shape is 'added' to the inside of the top, or end-piece, of the object, probably a 'spear-thrower', in the right hand of the figure of the First Twelfth. The pictograph of the 'flying-fish' of Tiahuanaco was based on a real zoological specimen, not on a figure of fancy of the type of the Greek Pegasus, or the winged bull of the Babylonians, or the Jewish flying camel (Cf. also Note 59.) Pictographs of the flying fish occur also on other remains of the classical period of Tiahuanaco.

[78] Reckoned from the probable level of the Ocean after the breakdown of the Satellite; reckoned from the sea-level of the present Age of Luna the uplift is only some 12,000 feet. (Cf. also note 32.)

[79] It goes without saying that the axis of the girdle-tide did *not* coincide with the terrestrial equator, but its situation was determined by the orbital plane of the Satellite, which certainly also showed a tilt relative to the equatorial plane of the Earth, like our Moon.

[80] With the exception of Posnansky, Bennett, and Kiss, all other writers on Tiahuanaco (cf. Bibliography) have only stayed among the ruins for very short periods. Even Stuebel, who spent nine years in South America, surveyed Tiahuanaco only for seven days.

[81] That important and exciting discoveries may be made when even only a few feet of soil are removed is proved by Bennett finding, in 1932, inside the 'Old Temple', a gigantic, beautifully sculptured monolithic statue, which Posnansky has now placed into a sort of Open Air Museum of Antiquities from Tiahuanaco at La Paz. It measures about 24 feet, by 3½ feet wide and thick and weighs about twenty tons. The statue, evidently that of a great deity, certainly dates from the First Period, but was worked over and adorned with a bas-relief of glyphs in the Second.

Index

INDEX

Mexico, 24, 174
migrations, 24, 33f
Minchin, Lake, 14
mines, prehistoric, 38
moat, 35, 177
models of buildings, 70
Mohammedan calendar, 153
monolithic building elements, 44, 51
monolithic gateways, 86, 87, 107, 119, 161, 179
monolithic statues, 64, 186
month, length of, 22, 23, 89, 91, 104f, 119
Moon, fate of, 18f
Moon, genesis of, 18f
moonless aeon, 25, 79, 179
Morkill, Lake, 67
mortises and tenons, 50, 52
moulds for casting, 70
myths, 27, 41, 42, 72, 78, 81, 178

nadiral tide-hill, 22
New Guinea, 24
non-numerical symbols, 116–119, 126
numerical symbols, 109–116, 122

Old Temple, 29, 30, 32, 35, 53, 63, 64, 68, 186
Ollantay-Parubo, fortress of, 66
Ollantay-Tambo, monastery of, 67
one day month, 23, 104f
operational symbols, 109, 116ff
orbital involution, 19ff, 105, 106, 174
orientated buildings, 28, 34, 75, 185
ornamental symbols, 109, 118f
ornamentation, 30, 35, 37, 182
ornithoid winged figures, 129f, 181, 185

Pacific Ocean, 23
Palace of the Red-White-Black Stairs, or Palace of the Sarcophagi, 42, 51, 54

palaeo-hydrography, 15
Parana, river, 74
Peru, 28, 57, 64, 82, 169
piedras cansadas, 39, 177
pointers, 37, 93, 94, 95, 96, 101, 115, 121, 124, 148, 181, 184, 185
polychromous pottery, 36, 178, 181, 182
polylithic gateway, 46, 48, 176
Poöpo, Lake, 13, 14, 15, 56, 57, 58, 73, 76, 174
Posnansky, Arthur, 36, 54, 91, 131, 169, 170, 175, 176, 179, 182, 184, 185, 186
Post-Diluvial Inter-Andean Sea, *see* Inter-Andean Sea, Post-Diluvial
potato, wild, 178
pottery, 36, 55, 65, 70, 74, 77, 164, 177, 178, 179, 180, 182, 186
precession of the Earth's axis, 174f, 181
precessional wobble, 24, 31, 33, 69, 71, 175, 185
prehistoric mines, 38
Pre-Titicaca, Lake, 13, 14, 28, 30, 31, 32
puma, 181, 182f
Puma Punku, 48, 51, 176, 177, 179, 180
puma star, 36, 77

quay walls, 53, 56
Quechua, 41, 81, 174, 175, 179, 181
Quimsachata, hill of, 30, 40
quipus, 116

racial types, 34
refugees, 24, 29, 33, 162, 165
refuges, 22, 24, 28, 73, 82
revolutions of satellite, apparent, 91, 106, 120ff, 125, 126, 133, 134, 145, 158

190

NOTE TO THE READER

Diagram 23, The Solar Year Part of the Tiahuanaco Calendar, appeared in earlier printings of this work as a large four-page fold-out. It was not possible to recreate that format in this printing, but in order to maintain the level of detail which the reader should see, it has still been reproduced close to its original size, which appears in a separated form over the next three pages, along with its original introductory notation.

Following these pages appears a minimized copy of the diagram on a single page, in order to show it in its complete, connected form.

The Publisher

DIAGRAM 23

THE SOLAR YEAR PART OF THE TIAHUANACO CALENDAR

The length of the great meander is 8 ft. 4 in., its height 7½ in. (Cf. Diagrams 14-18 which show some of the 'heads' in the bays of the meander in actual size.) The figure of the First Twelfth including its pedestal is 32 in. high (cf. also Diagram 19).

The numerals refer to the chronological succession of the Twelfths.

The panels of winged figures on either side of the First Twelfth and its pedestal (cf. Diagram 20) measure 24½ in. in height. They reach up slightly over the hands of the figure of the First Twelfth. The length of the panels coincides with the ends of the meander.

The diagram allows the appreciation of the balance of the design, of the fertility of conception, of the masterful meander, and of the sovereign certainty of lines and forms.

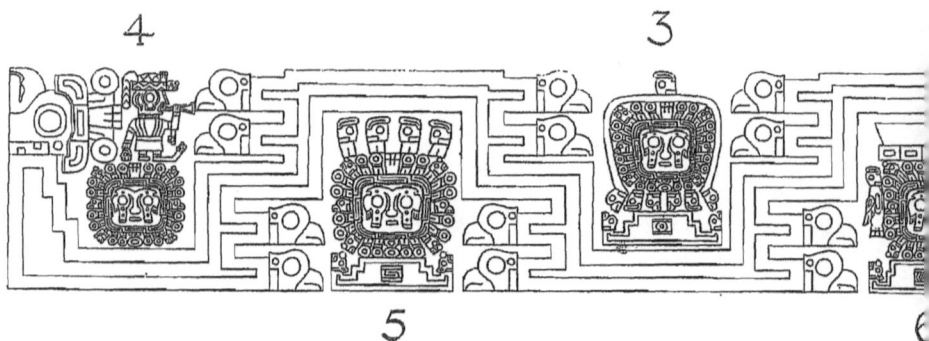

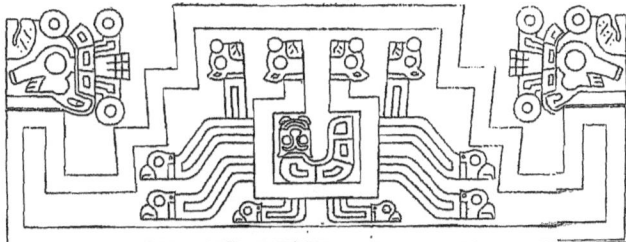

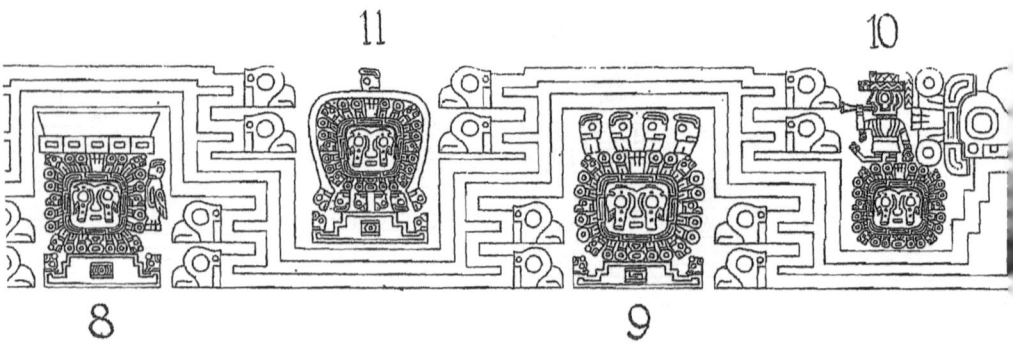

11

10

8

9

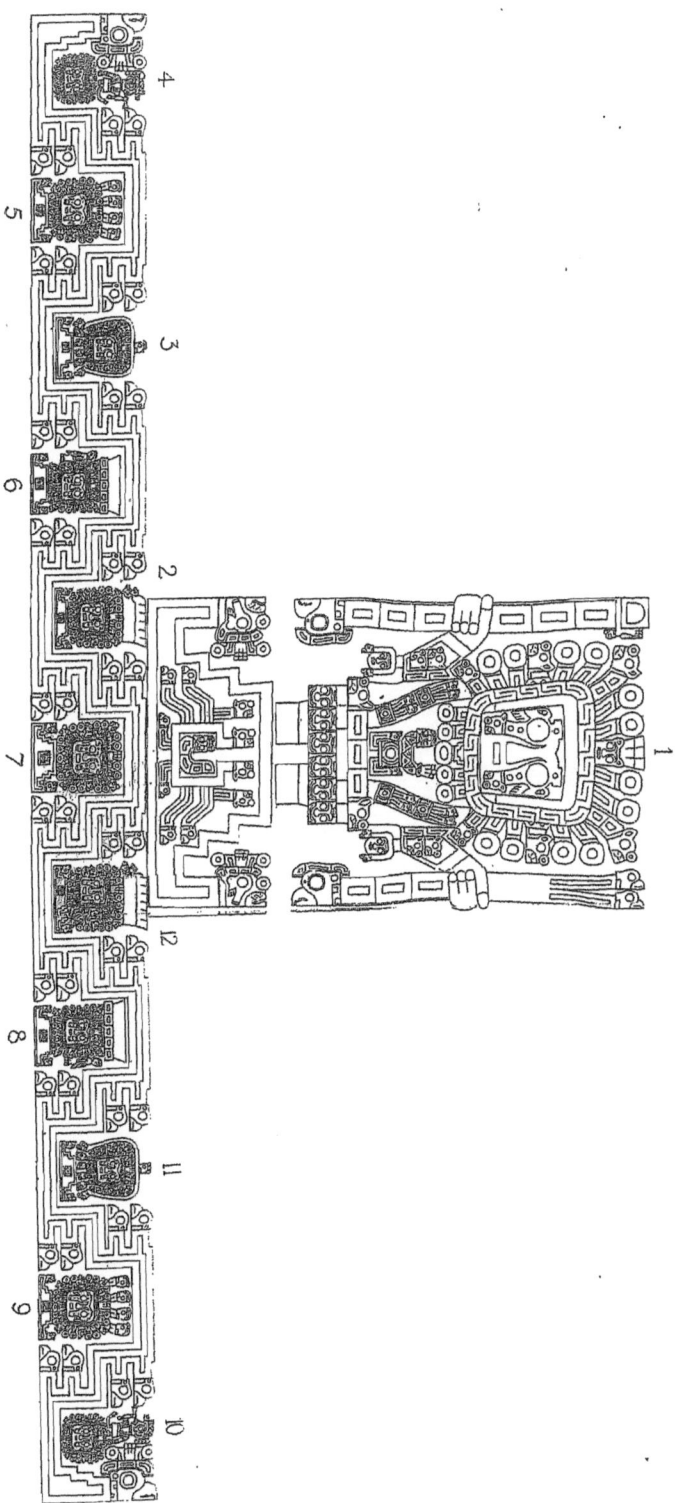